THE ART AND SCIENCE OF REAL ESTATE NEGOTIATION
SKILLS, STRATEGIES, TACTICS

The Real Estate Investor Manuals
Volume III

Gabrielle Dahms

Data provided here is deemed to be accurate but NOT guaranteed. The contents imply neither legal nor financial advice. Always thoroughly evaluate the facts relating to your specific circumstances. Neither do Booksmart Press LLC and/or Gabrielle Dahms guarantee success when applying this book's tactics and strategies. Readers should consult with appropriate professionals and do their homework. The author is not responsible for any liability, loss, or risk incurred resulting from the use of any of the information contained in this book -now or in the future.

All opinions and remaining spelling or grammatical mistakes are those of the author.
This is a non-fiction work.

Book Cover by Les

Published by Booksmart Press LLC

ISBN 13: 978-1-7331473-4-7 (print)
ISBN 13: 978-1-7331473-5-4 (ebook)
ISBN 13: 978-1-7331473-5-1 (audio book)

Publisher's Cataloging-in-Publication data
Names: Dahms, Gabrielle.
Title: The art and science of real estate negotiation / by Gabrielle Dahms.
Series: The Real Estate Investor Manuals
Description: Includes bibliographical references and index. | Cheyenne, WY: Booksmart Press, 2020.
Identifiers: ISBN: 978-1-7331473-4-7 (pbk.) | 978-1-7331473-5-4 (ebook) | 978-1-7331473-5-1 (audio)
Subjects: LCSH Real estate business. | Real property. | Real estate agents. | Negotiation in business. | House buying. | House selling. | Commercial real estate. | BISAC BUSINESS & ECONOMICS/ Real Estate / General | BUSINESS & ECONOMICS/ Negotiating | BUSINESS & ECONOMICS/ Conflict Resolution & Mediation
Classification: LCC HD1379 .D24 2020 | DDC 333.33--dc23

Other Books in This Series

How Trends Make You A Smarter Investor (Vol. I)

Finding Profitable Deals (Vol. II)

Upcoming book subjects in this series include:

    International real estate

    Affordable Housing

    Self-directed IRA real estate investment

    Market analysis

Paperback and hardcopy editions available from Ingram Sparks.

eBooks are available through eBook retailers, including Amazon, Apple, Barnes & Noble, Google Books, and many others.

Audio Book available starting December 2020.

Join our mailing list here

www.realestate-negotiation.com

We detest SPAM and do not send it.

All you receive are updates of our publications.

What Readers say about other books in the series

How Trends Make You A Smarter Investor

... this book was easy and entertaining to read - almost like a novel - quite an achievement in such a topic I would think of as "dry". Nonetheless Gabrielle Dahms covers the essential steps in real estate investment. The Real Estate Investing Manuals series takes a holistic approach to investment. – ✭✭✭✭✭ Kalavan

What I enjoyed most about this book is how the author was able to break down a complex subject into understandable terms and strategies. I have been a real estate agent for some time and know that real estate investment is a complicated process as there is so much to consider. In the The Real Estate Investing Manuals, Ms. Dahms was able to concisely and clearly explain all the steps. – ✭✭✭✭✭ L. Martini

This book has a wonderful section on 21st century topics in real estate, such as cryptocurrency, the gig economy and the opportunities it creates, and the current effects of technology in general on the real estate industry. I found the book's focus on how real estate shapes our society very interesting. For instance, it addresses green homes and community-focused real estate. - ★★★★★ D. Cale

Finding Profitable Deals

Many of us know that buying and selling real estate is a goldmine! The issue for me has been understanding the basics and where the deals are! So many real estate books I've picked up are sleepers! I just can't get through them. But not Gabrielle Dahms' book! I couldn't put it down! It was a fast and easy read and now, I am filled with inspiration and knowledge that I can use right now!! What a super resource!! Now I feel I'm on my way to Real Estate Wealth! – ★★★★★ Amazon customer

... very beneficial for those looking to just buy a family home. The author gives a surprising amount of information about what types of investments are out there. The author's insight makes me feel I can make the best purchase without the fear of losing my investment if I need to resell. I am looking forward to using the tips I learned to good use, thanks. - ★★★★★ J. Maxon

Dahms has a wealth of experience in this field and has even written about it previously on an extensive basis. If you are looking for a way to create passive income for life, this is the book for you. Not only is it about creating profitability, but doing your due diligence into a property, making sure it is the right fit for your circumstances. There are plenty of resources here to help you make an informed decision when it comes time to invest in real estate. Highly recommend. – ★★★★★ V. E.

DEDICATION

For all those who aim to be the best version of themselves: to my clients, friends and family.

TABLE OF CONTENTS

PREFACE

Negotiation took on new meaning when I traveled to Nepal to trek the Himalayas in 2016. The trek brought me in contact with a different world, one replete with new understanding. I interacted with many people in those gorgeous mountains. Most were gracious people. Living in the Himalayas equates to going back in time: inhabitants of ancient villages maintain the same lives their ancestors had centuries before them. They depend on yaks, their own two feet, hard physical labor, community, and ingenuity.

All the while those younger than thirty sported cell phones, one of the few modern inventions that has reached them. But far from the big cities, the Himalayan mountain people lead simple lives exposed to nature, its cycles, bounty, treachery, and beauty.

In contrast to the Nepali mountain people's lives, the trekking routes controlled by the Nepali government bring in the outside world, foreigners working out for fun and novelty. Those foreigners look different, speak other languages, and know luxury. They have much compared to the locals. The locals sell them food, candy, shawls and run guest houses along the route. All of them have uniform pricing and uniform menus, stipulated by the government. But some trekkers and tourists still feel they must haggle, a variant of negotiation.

After the trek, I explored Kathmandu. I imagined finding a Punjab pantsuit or have one tailored. The Thamel Marg, the ancient market labyrinth in the heart of Kathmandu, was sure to offer this. Off I went, weaving through narrow uneven streets, filled with shops and street vendors, passing innumerable stores selling dental protheses. This struck me as strange, as something I needed to know more about... But that is another story.

The streets and the market were alive. Many people pushed through their tight spaces, adding to the colorful mélange of spice vendors displaying their offerings of pots and pans, clothing and shoes, plastics and books dangling from makeshift carts or from rails in front of old buildings or carts. Dust and heat settled on all of them as they sat amid much left-over rubble from the big 2015 earthquake.

Most people in the market labyrinth were locals vying for wares. The few tourists were easily recognizable by tennis shoes, Teva sandals, backpacks, and cameras. Those tourists, me included, sported a distinct look, making it easy for vendors and beggars to solicit them to buy goods or for some money.

Everyone converged on the two major plazas, brought there via uneven alleys from all directions. My senses took in the colors, the dust, the garbage, the rubble, the ornate altars and temples in many corners, and the many offerings. The clothing that hung in plain view along the streets seemed cheaply made. It was nothing I wanted. Hoping to find better quality, I kept on, only to realize some time later that a novel approach was in order. But which approach?

The answer appeared before my very eyes, as if heaven sent. Two beautiful well-dressed Nepalese women, sisters, or friends perhaps, crossed my path. My gaze trailed them as they stopped at several stands, touching garments, and clearly discussing them. They appeared as dissatisfied with the wares as I was and suddenly dove into the tiniest entry in between stands, one I would never have seen on my own.

Aha, I thought, they are my ticket.

I arrived at the entry just as they turned a corner in what appeared to be a walkway, not much wider than a hiking trail, inside the building. I followed and saw diverging paths leading to various shops I would never have suspected there, small low-ceilinged catacomb-like rooms that had more access routes behind them. They seemed to go on endlessly into a world apart from that on the street, now only a few hundred meters behind me.

The women led me right to a tailor's shop, Shabu's shop, where the walls lined with shelves full of cloth, floor to ceiling. I found myself in a different world. The ladies had left their shoes at the entry. They sat on a small backless bench surrounded by pillows covering the entire floor, talking with the proprietor. Concentrating on their business, they did not notice me, but the cloth merchant shot me a quizzical look. Undeterred, I nodded in his direction and gestured that I had time and would wait.

What unfolded was worth the wait of about half an hour. Time did not seem to matter there. Barefoot, I seated myself on the cushioned floor while the tailor and the ladies had an animated leisurely conversation about various cloths which a young woman, either his wife or an assistant or both, brought upon request. The tailor clearly knew them.

They bantered about one particular cloth. Interested, the ladies exchanged glances, handled the cloth, handed it back. They vigorously shook their heads as he pointed out the fine points of the cloth by showing it off. This went on and on, and neither party appeared in any hurry. The headshaking intensified on both sides. Accompanied by serious faces, smiles, and silence.

Finally, the ladies got up, sweetly smiling at him, and walked out. I imagined them returning in a few days and picking up the threads of the negotiation that would bring them closer to owning the cloth, having it perfectly tailored and paying the right price.

While I will never know the outcome of their negotiations, I learned much about negotiating from them. Without understanding so much as one Nepali word, the lessons were priceless. They lent nuances to my own negotiation arsenal as a real estate broker and as an investor. They map across to everyday life issues and matters that require negotiation.

I then realized that although several excellent books on negotiation exist, only some address negotiating real estate. That is how this book took shape. Now, I hope you find it as interesting and valuable a tool to improve your negotiating skills and excel in them as I did writing it. I might even tell you about my own successful negotiation with the Nepali cloth merchant later on.

INTRODUCTION

Influence is when you are not the one talking and yet your words fill the room; when you are absent and yet your presence is felt everywhere. — Temitope Ibrahim.

In 2001 I apprenticed myself to a veteran San Francisco realtor® with over forty years of experience. Though I held a freshly minted California real estate license in hand, I realized that a license did not make me a real estate professional. Perhaps having grown up in Europe where apprenticeships carry high value saved me valuable time from floundering.

Learning the real estate business from a seasoned professional woman proved an excellent decision. This lady was one of the toughest negotiators I have ever known. Her clients were high-end, high-maintenance clients who expected no less. I consciously entered the world of negotiations and diplomacy under her tutelage and mentorship. I am grateful and remember one lesson in negotiation that dazzled me.

On one occasion, Ms. Jones[1] received a call from a buyer's agent on one of her listings. The agent asked aggressive questions, then told Ms. Jones a story about a perceived issue of the upscale property. She stated that her buyer wanted to renegotiate the already signed contract. She gave no other reasons but insisted the issue was real and that it had not been disclosed.

Ms. Jones, an attentive listener, took it all in and scribbled down notes. She did not interrupt, thanked the caller when she finished—and hung up the phone. She shot me a look across the room, asked me to bring her the voluminous property file and took a deep breath.

Her client, the seller, received a call from her only twenty minutes later. She briefly explained the situation and waited for his response. He evaded responding but stuttered out a few informative morsels. When he was complete, Ms. Jones

---

[1] All names of individuals, colleagues and clients have been changed to protect their identity and to maintain confidentiality.

said one brief sentence to her seller: "I can only help you if you are honest with me."

Silence ensued.

After what seemed a long time "alright, alright" followed. The seller laid the situation out for her. It turned out he feared that honesty about the undisclosed issue would have marred his property, netting him less. Ms. Jones reiterated his duty to disclose all known facts about the property. She also assured him she would negotiate hard for him. She started by telling the buyer's agent the truth. Then she ceded a small but important concession about the transaction's timing.

The buyer ended up leaving the contract in place. Why?

For several important reasons, the most important one of which was trust built upon good communication and integrity.

Not only the buyer and his agent walked away respected and satisfied. Some sellers would never have told their agent the truth, but Ms. Jones' authenticity, non-judgmental approach, and expertise transmitted to her client. He became a client for life and sent many referrals Ms. Jones' way.

Negotiating is an art and a science. Excellent negotiators are aware of this and hone their craft in both arenas. Whether you already are an excellent negotiator—in real estate or in another field—or whether you are a complete negotiation newbie, you likely appreciate the importance of negotiating well. You understand the importance of improving negotiations. Perhaps you already know that the ability to negotiate underlies everything you do in business and life. This spans deciding on a movie with your significant other, making sure your children complete their homework, or buying or selling a property.

The skill of negotiating nets desired results. Negotiation in its simplest form is communication aimed at reaching specific outcomes. It does not matter whether such outcomes are better terms, more money, getting a certain job, or consummating a real estate deal.

However, negotiations range from non-dollar items to multimillion-dollar transactions. They are nuanced, simple, yet complex. They involve people, circumstances, facts, resources, and many other moving parts and changing circumstances.

The history of negotiation is as old as mankind. The role of negotiation and diplomacy penetrate every life. Yes, diplomacy happens between regular people who are not ambassadors. Personality, mindset, attitude, vision, planning, preparation, and even courage define those who are masters.

The book's chapters set the stage for you to become a masterful negotiator versus shooting from the hip and operating by chance and luck. Topics presented include the role negotiations play in real estate transactions, how they influence them, and best practices to reach successful real estate agreements. Read an entire chapter about contracts, the true currency of real estate transactions.

Practical, the book aims to break through any pretenses. Simultaneously, it provides you, the reader, with negotiation fundamentals, strategies and tactics, common negotiating pitfalls, and ways to overcome any fears about negotiating. Find techniques, tips, a checklist, and other resources at your fingertips.

And one more thing: real estate transactions often involve large dollar amounts. And sizeable sums bring emotions to the surface. Most books written about negotiations in real estate focus on "analyze the numbers and base everything on them." While that approach is fine, it lacks the many nuances that enter any negotiation, including those in real estate.

The pages you are about to read contain what I have learned about real estate negotiating over the past twenty years. I refine aspects of these teachings every day. These pages then contain what I value, and how the knowledge, experience and expertise captured in them enriches me in my profession - and in my life.

The Art and Science of Real Estate Negotiation is specific to real estate, yet many of its topics are transferable to other areas of your life. If you, like many people, are now more than ever interested in the fascinating world of negotiations, read on.

I know that you may have read or are reading other books on the topic. That is great. I also know that learning to negotiate is trendy now. Many law firms and consultancies and prestigious universities offer negotiation courses and certificates.

Forever interested in the topic, I checked a few of these programs out. The Harvard Negotiation Project is one of them. Its name alone is prestigious, and its cost reflects this reality. Similar programs charge much money for knowledge, information and role playing.

Of course, it is wonderful if you attend one of these programs, but why not start with valuable information about negotiating that is specific to real estate and costs a fraction?

Especially when this book aims to add value to your real estate buying, selling, and investing. I wrote this book to empower you to be a better negotiator. Once you read the book, I hope you agree that you are getting much more than you paid for. Ready?

Go ahead, turn the page.

CHAPTER I

The charm of history and its enigmatic lesson consist in the fact that, from age to age, nothing changes and yet everything is completely different. – Aldous Huxley

A Quick Perspective

All of us negotiate every day. We have done so since the beginning of humankind. Negotiating in its simplest form is communication, even if business and politics define the term negotiation as we understand it. Negotiations span multiple parties that seek to find common ground to reach agreement. All are communications with the aim to reach an agreement and include diplomatic communication between nations. Negotiations are multidimensional, which is why power, leverage and creativity play big roles in them.

Naturally, real estate negotiation refers to business deals, and business deals appear to concern themselves with money. The word appear in the preceding sentence is a conscious choice. Most negotiations are about much more than money, even if money is their quantifiable measure.

Higher stakes distinguish any business negotiation from say, negotiating which movie to see or what to have for dinner. In business negotiations considerable amounts of money or other assets exchange hands. One or both parties benefit once they reach acceptable solutions and agree to them. However, on some occasions the outcome of a negotiation might be to arrive at no agreement.

Contrary to popular belief, reaching acceptable agreements is not all about dollars. Some property sellers want to ensure they are selling the property to the right party. Naturally, those sellers define the "right party" by what they believe that party must be. Even those who do not have this goal are influenced by the other party's conduct, that is by their treatment of them.

Subconscious and unconscious biases exist. This is true for property buyers and investors. Clearly, these are highly personal undertones. One important part of the art of negotiation is psychological. Another is reading between the lines. Yet another is putting all available information, including facts and figures, observations, and notations into their proper context. You get the idea.

Buying or selling real estate is no exception to the classic definition of negotiation. Either are business transactions. Either demand a wide range of skills, some of which are life skills. What sets real estate negotiations apart are the complexities of the negotiation process. To start, real estate negotiation most often involves more than two parties: the buyer, the seller, their representatives, inspectors, appraisers, title officers, mortgage professionals and banks, and the list goes on. This is often true even when no real estate professionals or attorneys represent sellers and buyers.

Real estate negotiations often are complex. Managing this complexity is part and parcel of negotiations. The items underlying all property negotiations are excellent communication, understanding timelines, contractual obligations, legal implications, and the large financial investment real estate requires.

Successful real estate negotiations follow certain sequences, timelines, requirements, preparations, economic or political leverage, back and forth, reviews, signings, and completions. They also have aftermaths in which buyers of sellers are happy with results, believe the other party fleeced them, or they would proceed differently, if given the chance.

Therefore, many negotiations have their own "half-lives." The parties' memories of the negotiation live on and influence future decisions. One consequence of negotiations is that parties may do business again or stay away from doing business with the other party.

Next, studies show that negotiating parties have biases either toward agreement or toward impasses. An impasse refers to a stalled or aborted negotiation. If an impasse occurs, it most often equals failure in the parties' minds. Further, whether the parties have a bias toward agreement or impasse often depends on how the offer is presented. Language plays a huge role. So does mindset. But I am getting ahead to myself...

As already mentioned, negotiating real estate implies identifying the right property or the right buyer for a property. Moreover, this requires a strategy, a plan, tactical know-how, asset and market knowledge, expertise, and other skills.

As in all fields, you can become a passable or even excellent negotiator by either learning from an accomplished negotiator, by reading books and taking courses, or by sheer experience. The latter option is less easy than it appears. Your time commitment and effort stand in direct proportion to which type of negotiator you will be. Sorry, there is no shortcut.

My master's in history proves an incredible tool in negotiating because history is full of brilliant strategists and negotiators. A few examples of them are part of the chapters. I hope you enjoy reading about them. Maybe they inspire you to immerse yourself in more reading or in learning from all people who cross your path. Consider including your children and those you do not yet see as negotiators.

While only some famous people who appear in these pages had any interest in real estate, this chapter describes two men who became wealthy through real estate. Some of you might immediately think of *The Art of the Deal*. Although I read it, the book's ghostwriter labeled it fiction, and it appears Mr. Trump implemented little the book presents. The book is a shining example of mistaken identity. It is also a public relations gig that looms large in the imagination. No other discussion of it follows.

Let's move on to John Jacob Astor (1763-1848) is synonymous with New York City. He immigrated to New York, then a small town, right after the American Revolution in 1784. Astor was a German immigrant whose family in Germany was poor. He was one of ten children. His family's poverty meant that the Astor children had to fend for themselves. John Jacob was no exception. At fifteen, he joined his brothers in London, became a musical instrument maker, anglicized his name, and learned English. His next voyage took him to New York, where he would join one of his brothers.

He met his wife Sarah Cox Todd when he rented a room from her mother. He remained in New York. His wife was an astute businesswoman with a network of social connections. Both benefitted him throughout his life.

For a while he worked in his brother's butcher shop. Eventually, his interest shifted to the fur-trading business, a business for which he eventually established a monopoly. The Jay Treaty between the United States and Britain in 1794 opened fur trading markets in the Great Lakes region and in Canada. He took advantage of that treaty and established the American Fur Company in 1808.

Although the American Fur Company has a colorful history at which I can only hint here, it became a monopoly in 1817 by absorbing its competitors. Yet, Astor foresaw the fur trading business' eventual decline long before it happened.

As a man who always hedged his bets, Astor bought real estate in Manhattan as early as 1799. New York was then a small town, but his assessment was that it would experience a boom and become one of the world's great cities. His thinking went like this:

From a fort you get a trading post, and from a trading post you will get a city.

His net worth was $20 million—over $600 million in today's dollars - when he died.

Astor was a shrewd negotiator who knew what he wanted. He excelled in establishing and maintaining relationships. His vision, creativity, business skills, negotiation skills, communication skills propelled him to riches. Note however, that he did not do so alone. His wife was an excellent business partner, and he relied on her regarding business details and running his affairs when he was away.

Some characteristics that made him a successful negotiator were that he was not afraid of change, and able to identify opportunities and act on them. He leveraged connections and relationships and believed in honesty and fairness in all his dealings.

Astor's characteristics in building a real estate empire are instructive. They map across to anyone wishing to do the same today. Keep them in mind.

The other man who made his fortune in real estate is Ray Kroc (1902-1984). I know you may immediately associate Ray Kroc with McDonald's, the ubiquitous American hamburger chain. You would be partially right.

McDonald's is its own business, a public company traded on the New York Stock exchange. The part you may not yet know is that Mr. Kroc viewed McDonald's as something other than hamburgers, fries, and milkshakes. Rather, he stated, "my business is real estate." This stemmed from his belief that the real estate where McDonald's franchises stand is much more valuable than either the structures on it or the hamburgers those franchise operations sell.

Mr. Kroc's business model therefore depended (it still does) on acquiring cheap property, usually along highways with many travelers traversing them. In 1956, Mr. Kroc therefore established *The McDonald's Franchise Realty Corporation* with that goal. The franchising model that followed was a natural outgrowth of this approach.

But the McDonald's story begins with Mr. Kroc's visit to the McDonald brothers who owned a thriving restaurant in San Bernardino, California. They sold fast food and milkshakes. Kroc, then a milkshake mixer salesman, had sold them several mixers. They impressed him with their ideas and business sense, and with their successful restaurant operation.

Kroc purchased the McDonald's franchise system and made them partners. The franchise model and the business had innumerable problems that ranged from franchise location, to cleanliness, to product consistency, to pricing. Although the partnership with Kroc made the McDonald brothers rich, strains also appeared in the relationship.

McDonald's franchises lease the land and the buildings to franchisees on a long-term basis. Franchisees pay rent, franchise fees, and royalty fees. The sales of burgers and fries predicate the rent franchisees pay. In theory, all this landlord needs to do is collect those proceeds per contractual agreement.

It is easy to see that this long-term lease business depends on contracts that cover all bases. Note that this is a different model than being a landlord of, say, a 6-unit apartment building.

McDonald's makes money whether or not the franchisee generates sales. By contrast, the 6-unit apartment building landlord only makes money when tenants occupy the apartments. Mr. Kroc and now the McDonald's Corporation are masters of this business model.

Talk about creating cashflow!

Ray Kroc built his real estate empire by being a keen observer, by identifying opportunities, by leveraging relationships, by holding a vision, and by knowing what he wanted. He treated business associates, suppliers, and his customers fairly and had an aversion to gauging customers. He believed in and advocated the pioneer spirit. Integrity, high standards and rigor were top of mind for Kroc. This quote from him is most instructive for all real estate buyers and sellers:

If you work just for money, you'll never make it, but if you love what you're doing and you always put the customer first, success will be yours.

Something important to note before we jump into the content is that you will see fewer acclaimed and known women negotiators in all fields of human endeavor. Cultural and social norms are the primary reasons for this lopsided picture. Excellent women negotiators clutter the field of history, but few ever received acknowledgement. If they received acknowledgement, it was often as martyrs or saints. Such labels remove their abilities and ascribe them to a nefarious source. More common is the view that brilliant women negotiators are self-serving, power hungry, dragon ladies, and even "nasty" women. Such views, often subtle and subconscious, persist today.

Of course, this begs the question whether they behaved differently than their male counterparts. Possibly so, but unlikely. They stood out as brilliant negotiators, something considered the purview of men.

The assumption and accusation are that something is wrong with them, meaning they do not abide by the cultural precept of the subservient woman of their times. The expectation of many cultures continues to be for women to serve others, especially their husbands, even today. Thus, many women's negotiating skills are ignored or discounted. And women mask their accomplishments and watch men co-opt them as their own.

Dolores Huerta, co-founder of the United Farm Workers and an accomplished and tough contract negotiator, the puts this phenomenon like this:

I started really noticing, more and more, how men will plagiarize and take credit for women's work... I have noticed that it just happens a lot.

Keep this interesting and persistent disparity in mind as you read this book, especially if you are—like me—a woman. If you are a man, notice the phenomenon and resist it in your next negotiation.

You may already see that negotiating is an art and a science. Excellent negotiators are aware of this and hone their craft in both arenas. You may well be an excellent negotiator—in real estate or in another field. Or you may be a complete negotiation newbie. In either case, I imagine you appreciate the importance of negotiating well.

Perhaps you know that the ability to negotiate underlies everything you do: from minor items, to relationships, to buying a car, to buying a home, to fulfilling your dreams, to helping those you love, your community and society.

The idea and aim of this book are to give you the best possible starting point if you are a beginner. If you are an accomplished negotiator, the book may help you approach the subject from a fresh vantage point.

CHAPTER II

The consequences of our actions are the scarecrows of fools and the beacons of wise men. — T.H. Huxley

Negotiating Fundamentals I

If you have ever watched real estate reality shows like House Hunters, Million-Dollar Listing, Flip or Flop, Fixer-Upper or any others, you probably have an idea about negotiations as being though and dramatic. Perhaps you believe that you are going into a kind of war were only one party wins, usually by any means necessary.

Even though some of these shows relish glamor, flair and drama, they portray the other party as an adversary, someone they cannot and will not trust someone to vanquish. And this makes sense for entertainment value, but it bears little semblance to reality.

Successful negotiations depend on parties respecting and trusting each other. This stands in stark contrast to considering the other party an adversary. The TV reality strategy works on TV and in the viewer's imagination but in actual life it hardly ever leads to successful agreements, the outcomes for which negotiations aim.

For this reason, the first and foremost underlying principle to remember is that negotiations rely on engaging the other party, possibly persuading them to your point of view—both through meticulous research and through understanding human nature.

Seeking to understand the other party usually nets successful results, and that is true even when disagreements between the parties exist. This approach stands in contrast with the idea that one enters negotiations to get what one wants. Making friends is not usually on people's minds when they think about negotiating.

Yet, one of the most important components of successful negotiations is to establish a friendly and even harmonious connection with the other party. That is rapport. Briefly put, when rapport is present, the parties respect and trust each other. This allows the parties to engage in a meaningful dialogue, to understand each other, to seek solutions that work for both, and to maintain long-term relationships. Long-term relationships are imperative in uncovering and future opportunities. That alone could be extraordinarily profitable.

Rapport underlies all human transactions, whether those are negotiations or everyday relationships. It is psychologically powerful because it is about the other party wanting you to succeed, something that usually happens if they like you. When rapport exists, options and opportunities present themselves and negotiations become about seeking true agreements. When rapport doesn't exist, negotiations become purely transactional, "all business," antagonistic, and warlike. In the latter case, the loser often feels slighted and even angry, retribution on his mind.

By now you probably see the benefits of rapport and how it can make a difference in real estate negotiations and in all relationships. You probably also understand that rapport is an attitude, of mindset, and approach that requires ongoing effort. It is about building relationships, about people. And negotiations are people interacting with people to reach an agreement. People can give you what you want. This works both ways. It is a two-way street.

In all my years in real estate, the transactions in which the parties had mutual trust and respect often were also those in which solid agreements happen. They are also those that led to long-term relationships, buyers, sellers, and investors. Often, those parties continued to do business with each other over and over. This clearly is valuable in and of itself, considering that parties who lack rapport lose opportunities. They often must start over again and again.

Incidentally, Barbara Corcoran, the legendary founder of *The Corcoran Group* and TV reality show personality of the *Shark Tank*, understands rapport well. Even though her philosophy is to pressure the other party, she knows that respect engenders loyalty. Any pressure then is to move the transaction forward versus antagonizing the other party.

Add to this her marketing genius and the fact that she wants to *be the name on people's lips*, something that can only result from people liking and trusting her and her company. This also goes together with her take on trusting your gut, which is another component that is only possible by paying close attention to who the other party is and what they need and desire.

Now let us put this into the context of everything being negotiable, no matter what it is. Life is about negotiating and negotiating is about life. The more you understand about life and take an active part in it, the better your negotiation skills will grow. If that seems counter intuitive, read on.

As already mentioned, many of us think about negotiations as winning at any cost and even to wipe out the other party. While those types of negotiations exist, they are short-sighted and less desirable than navigating a larger field, where everybody concerned gains something. That is even true when negotiations cannot reach the agreement stage.

In addition, the view of negotiating as adversarial has two other effects. One of them is the fear of negotiating, often expressed in statements like "I don't know how to negotiate" or" I'm not a good negotiator" or" I don't like negotiating." Many variations of the theme exist, and you will hear some creative ones when you listen to conversations about just about any topic. - The other effect is a "winner take all" approach, which sounds good on the surface, but which is a declaration of war on the other party. In this approach, power, ego, and sheer force of will often trump common sense rather than finding a workable solution with long-term benefits for all parties involved.

The big drawback of this approach is that the one who takes all is most often despised and the other party seeks retribution. This is true in all contexts: nations at war, divorce cases, heirs haggling about their inheritance, professionals who disappear instead of fulfilling their obligations to their clients, estate transactions, and the list goes on.

Although every party comes with its own unique culture, but you can bypass any differences by appealing to self-interest. According to Robert Greene in *The 48 Laws of Power* self-interest is a language that all of us speak and understand.

One key step in the process is to understand the other party's psychology. What traits and concerns do they display? Who are they in terms of social standing, status, credentials, or perceived credentials? Is it money, greed, or power, or both, or something else that motivate them? Are they patient or impatient, prone to anger and outbursts, impetuous? Are they self-important? Do they want to avoid conflict altogether? Or maybe they wish to be charitable merciful and just or appear that way?

Many negotiations include flattering the other party. Some people want to show their good intentions and heart. Give them that opportunity once you have identified that this is what moves them. But if you see that a party's motivation is greed, yet appeal to a more noble motives which they care nothing about, they will not move your direction. The reverse is also true.

Knowing the other party's motivation will help you with strategy and tactics. One of the most important first actions you can take is to find out how to meet the other party's needs and how to help advance their cause. In doing so, see whether you can enter the other person's mind and observe their needs and interests. Also aim to get rid of your own feelings because they obscure the truth.

In that same vein, know with whom you are dealing. This is especially important because sometimes people take on different roles and confusion ensues. Assess people's honesty, loyalty, patience, flexibility, and even their breaking point. If you know any of these or, better yet, all of them, you will be able to predict the party's actions.

All people have their own culture and the culture of their tribe and community, the culture of their background, and the culture of their country and so on. These cultural parameters, while varying from person to person, coalesce and create the norms and standards by which that person abides. For starters, know your own and understand them, then seek to understand those of the other party. Doing this will also help you understand that nothing is personal.

Traits of negotiators include self-discipline, persistence, assertiveness, instinct, curiosity, creativity, humility, courage, the ability to listen, and the ability to communicate and to persuade. Negotiators also must understand and be able to interpret facts and numbers. They must be able to navigate a complex process that involves different parties, goals, and solutions. Excellent negotiators solve problems for themselves and for others because they know that problems and challenges contain abundant opportunities.

Negotiation is as much about the personalities that negotiate with one another as it is about the aim of the negotiation. Assiduously study yourself and the other party and before you enter any negotiation. Know the other party's and your own negotiation style, whether it is collaborative (win win), accommodating (I lose, you win), competitive (I win, you lose), seeking compromise (we both win some and lose some), or one of avoidance (lose-lose).

All these negotiation styles are distinct from one another. They derive from different mindsets and use different strategies. They often result in different outcomes. Parties might become more and more antagonistic which is often the case in competitive negotiations– or seek compromise. Other parties yet seek to avoid conflicts altogether. Interestingly, conflict avoidance often leads to aggression where conflict escalates and neither party backs down. The result here are tough negotiations that take expertise to defuse.

Negotiations range from easy to difficult to impossible. If a party feels taken advantage of, they either walk away or make implementation painful. Most parties who negotiate want fair treatment, want to get or to pay a fair price, and to get value. Although the concept of fairness is subjective and an overused one at that, it remains important in negotiations. Understanding what fairness means to the other party is part of the homework and due diligence needed.

In property negotiations, fairness shows up almost right away. Sellers who may have bought their homes or properties forty years ago for little money, today want to sell that property or fair market value and/or a fair price. This is completely legitimate because what a party paid for their property has no bearing on what the property is worth today.

And property buyers aim to pay a fair price, the basis for which usually is the market value of the property. They dislike overbidding or paying more than market value. In fact, most buyers aim to purchase properties slightly below market. I am purposefully leaving out those buyers who believe that they ought to get a market value property for a fraction of what it is worth. While that sounds wonderful, it is unrealistic, and such buyers often waste much time, energy, and effort on this goal.

Finally, some property investors seek to pay a fair price for the promise of future income. And other property investors want to pay below market prices to factor in improving properties. That may mean they invest in rehabbing (renovating) properties, often also known as fix and flip, and rezoning and or developing the property, or in upgrading property to increase income potential. Many variations on this theme exist, but the salient feature of property investing rests on adding value that creates profits.

Knowledge of the other party is as important as knowledge of self. In case lack of knowledge in either prevails in negotiations, they are likely to get off to the wrong start and to the wrong conclusion. Similarly, if you are in a rush, have a cluttered mind, e.g. no focus or easily succumb to bait, you will miss important signs or mistake them for something else, have an insecure foundation and be unlikely to complete transactions.

When you are and remain focused, prepared, attentive, patient, flexible, you will be open to unexpected opportunities that inevitably arise in all negotiations. And when they do, you will be able to take advantage of them.

Let us briefly address the adage "time is of the essence." Time and timely performance are essential components of any contract, which also define successful negotiations. Every party has their own timing, though negotiation and the agreement usually have strict timelines. The other party might attempt to upset the timing of the negotiations by acting impatient and wanting to hurry things along or by being exceedingly slow and making you wait. Knowing this, resolve to stay patient no matter what happens.

Negotiation deadlines and contract deadlines impose timing that affects all parties. Such deadlines put pressure on the parties. When there is pressure either through lack of time or lingering in limbo, mistakes happen. But that can change quickly and suddenly, and a negotiation that seems to sit in limbo can move to a frenetic pace. The best course of action is to prepare and plan for either circumstance to meet it.

As you can see, negotiating is an art and a science. It is a practice which requires continuous refinement, attention, interest, and dedication. It is the practice of becoming a masterful persuader, of leveraging one's own natural negotiation style, inducing the spirit of cooperation among the parties, navigating the stages, and masterfully handling difficult people and situations.

Negotiation is not manipulation. While some parties and people manipulate others, usually with short-term tactics designed to do so but sometimes with lies and trickery, manipulation tends to backfire. It is also dishonest, unethical, and unprofessional.

It no doubt counts to do what you promised. Fulfill your promises and obligations. You will build your reputation positively if you do, negatively if you do not. In either case, word will travel about how you treated the other party. Although you may not even be aware of how others perceive you and your business, the reputation others attribute to you precedes you in your endeavors. In fact, your reputation will affect your business, if not right away, so certainly down-the-line. Always stay aware of this.

This point is so important that it bears repeating: negotiations start before you ever come to the table with the other party. It literally pays to get to know the other party, their desires, requirements, and needs Yes, this may sound counterintuitive, but it will bear plentiful fruit if used authentically, engagingly, and with a beginner's mind.

Always remember this in both your personal and professional life. If you want to make money, make this the one thing remember first, the thing to do first, and always pay attention to it. Do not worry about those who ridicule you for it. They might be parties that turn out to be inappropriate or undesirable to deal with, at any rate.

A transaction I represented the buyers in illustrates some of these points.

Several years ago, a professional mid-thirties married couple came to me by referral. The couple was lovely. They knew what they wanted. We hit it off and found the perfect property for them within a short time. It was a full flat Edwardian condo with modern bells and whistles, views, and a great location. Aside from this, the building was in excellent shape and the seller motivated. After having done our homework, they signed the contract to purchase this property for almost $2 million.

We had discussed the price point and their financial wherewithal before making the offer, especially because they had a specialty loan offered by only one lender. However, their desire for this property was so strong that they ignored my advice to have a financial backup plan in place and told me it would all work out just fine.

Everything appeared to be going along just fine. We did our inspections, reviewed the disclosures, addressed any other issues that could have hindered the transaction. Their lender, however, was out of state and did not understand San Francisco real estate. The lender also seemed to have a piecemeal process in place. As the finance contingency timeline drew to a close, my communications with the lender intensified and the mortgage professional gave us the go-ahead to remove the contingency.

Unfortunately for us, the lender's underwriting department, unbeknownst to us, had not done its job. One fine Saturday afternoon, I received a call from the bank's underwriting department, not from the mortgage broker. The underwriter stated that the current building insurance was insufficient. The call came four days after we had removed the loan contingency. That meant my clients could be on the hook for the three percent earnest money if unable to close the deal. The contract's liquidated damages clause specified as much.

My calls and my clients' calls to the mortgage professional went unanswered. We only heard from her once more via email. She took no responsibility for dropping the ball.

After a long conversation with the listing agent, he advised the seller to get the necessary insurance on the building. Then it turned out that the seller had no interest in doing so because he was a partner in a property insurance company that did not offer such a policy. He had no desire to get an insurance policy with a different insurer! He refused to get the insurance that the lender required!

Meanwhile, my clients' earnest money was at risk because we had removed all contingencies before this situation arose. I explained the situation to them and put them in touch with other local lenders.

They refused to even get in touch with those other lenders because none of them would offer them the specialty loan they wanted. Instead, this couple hedged their bets on their original lender, the one who had already deserted them. They believed their mortgage professional would come back to the table and would deliver. Neither they nor I ever received any return call from that mortgage professional. Last I heard, she is still in business.

This, of course, is where the plot thickens because now my clients' earnest money was at risk. Per the contract, they stood to lose it. I started the conversation about the circumstances and the earnest money with the listing agent. Intense negotiations ensued. In the end, the seller agreed to keep only twenty percent of the earnest money and to release the other eighty percent.

This saved my clients a tremendous amount of money for breaching the contract by not being able to deliver. But my clients were not happy and now claimed that I had failed to negotiate hard enough for them. This claim was unfounded and originated with the wife. She believed herself to be an excellent negotiator.

She suddenly began a push to speak with the seller directly, antagonizing all parties: the seller, the listing agents and myself. Even her husband disagreed with her but dared not say so. She put all of us on the defensive.

Another stressful week went by and the listing agent and I finally gave up, putting her in direct contact with the seller. I stayed away from being party to that conversation. The buyer apparently talked his ear off, but at this point the seller was so teed off that he dug in his heals. He now would only agree to release fifty percent of the earnest money. That meant an additional thirty percent on top of the original twenty percent I had negotiated!

What happened was completely unnecessary. This buyer whittled away goodwill with antagonism, an additional thirty percent of her and her husband's money, destroyed trust, respect and relationships. It was a sad day, but in the real estate business you see it all. I decided not to pursue the commission she owed me, mainly because I had no interest in prolonging the "relationship" through legal proceedings. Neither she or her husband ever thanked me.

What you just read encapsulates everything discussed and the glorious thing is that there are other deserving and appreciative real estate buyers, sellers, and investors out there. I am fortunate to count many of them as my clients.

Read the report above as a heads up about what can happen when unreliable partners and ego enter the field. Instead, focus on creating and establishing rapport and remain vigilant when circumstances deteriorate.

Consider this short list:

- Be your authentic self.

- Smile.

- Listen.

- Empathize.

- Engage.

- Tell the truth.

- Be polite.

- Think before speaking.

- Modulate your voice.

- Consider cultural nuances.

- Some cultures are relationship oriented; others are results or task oriented.

- Consider communication styles.

- They may be direct or indirect.

A real estate negotiation comprises many parties: buyers, sellers, investors, realtors®, attorneys, mortgage professionals, contractors, inspectors, title reps, and others. These parties influence the real estate transaction and how it transpires.

Although not all these parties are visible, they are part of the negotiation process. A normal real estate transaction involves as many as thirty different parties. Most of the time realtors® communicate with almost all of them and negotiate issues that arise from pertinent information, disclosures, and written and verbal communication. Disclosure documents represent only a minor component of this. The process is much larger.

For this reason, the real estate professionals involved in a real estate transaction ought to be excellent negotiators and hone their skills every day. Aside from their fiduciary duties to the client they represent, they write and execute real estate contracts, which come into play when the parties reach agreement. This is true even though most of them are not lawyers and therefore cannot dispense legal advice.

Next, it is important to understand that at times the players at the negotiation table are invisible. This is often the case in large commercial real estate transactions, when sellers, buyers or investors are banks, institutions, or government agencies. It may turn out that who you think you are dealing with is entirely different from the decision maker.

Make sure to a consider this and find out everything you can during your information finding phase. Also, ensure you know who the decision maker is and whether processes and procedures which differ from other real estate transactions are in place.

Challenges arise during negotiations. Among the things that can happen are:

- Anger.

- Hostility from the other party.

- New demands from the other party.

- Silence

- Partial responses.

- New players entering the field.

- Negotiations cease.

- The deal is dead

In any of the foregoing scenarios, one mistake can cost dearly. However, mistakes are human. They happen. Therefore, it is less about whether mistakes happen and much more about how to address them when they do. Parties reveal themselves, their motivations, personas, no matter where the mistake originates. It matters how you deal with that situation. This sounds easy, yet it is often rather difficult.

Excellent negotiators never shoot from the hip. Instead, they think a great deal before acting. They consider all facets, as well as their obligations, duties, and their inclinations. They analyze the situation, consider what it requires and above all, they remain calm. They also know that although everything is negotiable, not everything is worth negotiating.

Still, once they decide, they proceed without looking back. If their decision is wrong, they take responsibility and start again, wisdom gained. If their decision is right, they win and they gain. In either case, they persevere.

When negotiating real estate transactions, the parties may arrive at agreement which they then might renegotiate throughout the transaction. For example, if an inspection report reveals structural problems unknown when signing the contract, the buyer may ask the seller to make the needed repairs or to lower the price.

Be aware that some buyers suddenly ask for much more than the inspection report warrants. This is a poor business practice that puts the other party on the defensive. Buyers should never use inspection reports in this way. Their agents should not allow them to do so, either. When renegotiating in this scenario, neither party should get more nor less than the inspection report shows. The goal is to make the parties whole, not to take advantage of them.

Other circumstances might warrant ending negotiations, either for good or allowing the parties to start fresh. Frankly, I ought to have ended negotiations in the liquidated damages scenario you read about earlier in this chapter.

The reason is that one buyer turned aggressive, belligerent, and unappreciative. On top of that she demanded that the seller forego the entire liquidated damages amount. She also blamed me for the financing issues, probably because her mortgage broker disappeared and hid behind the large legal department of her bank. Instead of walking away, I learned a valuable, if stressful, lesson that cost me many hours and income.

Alas. Other reasons to walk away from negotiations include buyers who impose excessive demands. For instance, buyers who ask for a long list of minor repairs versus the bigger structural repairs home inspections reveal. Another example is a buyer who asks for the seller's personal property as part of the sale. Yes, appliances are personal property and those usually come with the property, but other personal property does not.

Other reasons to end negotiating with the other party might arise when you cannot confirm the buyer's proof of funds. That may mean the buyer has either no funds or insufficient funds to consummate the transaction. Regarding funds, buyers who fail to transfer the earnest money into escrow by the contract timeline send a big red flag.

And then there are appraisal issues. For instance, an appraisal that comes in at a higher or lower value than the accepted offer price. In the case of the higher appraisal, the buyer must have funds to pay the difference between the accepted offer price and the higher appraised value. Note that this applies to loans and that lenders will require buyers to do so.

Also know that if the appraisal comes in lower than the accepted offer price, the seller can either lower the accepted offer price or cancel the contract. Buyers will often ask for a lower price. Renegotiating the deal may work fine for both parties, but if the seller cannot afford to lower the price, walking away is something to consider. If you are a seller in this situation, you must make sure that canceling the contract is the right course of action because finding another buyer may prove difficult. Discuss these options with your real estate professional or with an attorney.

You might already see another problem, which is that some buyers have no funds to follow suit. In that case, cancel the contract and walk away. The buyers will not owe you anything if all these items show up during the appraisal and loan contingency period. Preferably tie together those two contingency dates.

Talking about lowering the price, some buyers submit lowball counteroffer after lowball counteroffer. This communicates several things. The buyers either have no agent or they are not listening to their agent. Either way, the market environment makes a tremendous difference when looking at lowball offers. If selling the home in a buyer's market, the buyers have options. In that case, it is best to counter their lowball offer with the amount for which you would sell the home. That may be lower than the listing price or not.

Clearly, sellers have more leverage in a seller's market. You could simply insist on the list price. However, if a buyer lowballs you in a seller's market, other factors are at work. You must evaluate whether to make a concession instead of lowering the price. The concession must be something the buyer values and wants. For example, a seller could pay for some needed repairs or adjust escrow timelines.

Sellers also do well to remind themselves why they are selling because that could influence the price or the terms. Does getting the highest price outweigh selling as fast as possible and vice versa? Does the market the property is in justify adjustments?

Sometimes sellers' emotions also get in the way because they believe their property is something special. Maybe so, but even if this is true, it is best to take out these emotions.

— Still, lowball offers could also send a signal that the buyer will be difficult to deal with and sellers have the option to cancel the transaction.

Some buyers also attempt to exert power over the seller by threatening to walk away from the negotiations and the deal. Threatening the other party once and putting pressure on them might be completely legitimate. However, if similar threats regularly appear, working with this buyer is likely to be difficult and unpleasant. In that case, sellers and their agents may wish to assess whether it is better to wait for a different buyer.

We have already covered much ground in this chapter. If there is nothing else, you get from it, understand this: the present and the future heavily rely on communication skills, on creativity, and on collaboration. Monetary gains, people who support you - another valuable resource never to underestimate -, and your reputation flow from those skills and abilities.

Therefore, look out for others' interests as if they were your own. Asking "what's in it for me" is perfectly fine and legitimate and what most people think about first but make it a habit to understand the other party's interests. Think of doing so as a guarantee for generating return on investment (ROI).

For example, find out whether there are specific terms the other party needs. Perhaps they are downsizing or retiring. Perhaps they need a specific contingency. Find out their circumstances without prying. One way to do this is to ask sellers or their agent how long they have lived in the property or how long they have owned it. You can then deepen that conversation and present what you or the party you represent might bring to the table.

In the time of COVID-19, it is more difficult and cumbersome to meet the other party in person. If it is at all possible, in-person meetings can be important to real estate negotiations. Sometimes they are indispensable. Even if it is not possible to meet in person, do your best to "put a face" on any offer you make as a buyer or an investor. Sometimes writing a personal letter, delivered alongside your offer, makes the difference.

If all this seems overwhelming, it need not be. Ask for help from people more knowledgeable than yourself and from those who possess real estate knowledge. They often also have a network of other professionals, which is to your benefit. If you are wondering how to find these individuals, read the other titles in this series. Engage the right professionals and develop your own negotiating muscle while you do so. It will serve you well in real estate transactions and in other areas in your life.

CHAPTER III

Few things are brought to a successful issue by impetuous desire, but most by calm and prudent forethought. — Thucydides

Negotiation Fundamentals II

The Negotiation Process

Think of the negotiation process as a recipe. If you bake a cake, the recipe guides you. It lists the ingredients, viable substitutes, the method of assembling the ingredient, the order in which to add them. Once the batter is ready, it must transform into a delicious fragrant cake. This requires an oven, the right temperate and the right baking time. Only then is there a cake.

Some of you great bakers out there remark just about now that other variables exist — down to the pan. And if we were to put ten bakers into the same room and to ask them to bake the same cake, the cakes would be slightly different because each baker lends the cake a distinct personal style. One baker might refine the cake by adding cinnamon instead of cardamom, etc. Another might lessen the amount of sugar. A third one might bake it gluten-free. You get the idea, even if I present it in the simplest way.

Negotiations follow a process, one which underlies all negotiations, and whose aim is agreement between the parties. What follows summarizes this process. Naturally, it is possible to leave out some steps and still come to an agreement, just as it is possible to leave out some ingredients when baking a cake. But at least some ingredients or steps are essential. One trick is to work out which ones and when.

And just like with a cake, even the slightest change might produce a different outcome. The cake either might be inedible or the most delicious cake ever. For negotiations, results could be truncated unsuccessful negotiations and agreements or reaching agreements that culminate in consummating deals.

The steps of the process precede the actual negotiation. When most people think of negotiation, they think of bargaining, of the back and forth between the parties. The previous chapter examined rapport building, communication styles, and negotiation styles. This chapter builds on what you read there.

To simplify, the steps in the process are identifying a property of interest, due diligence, planning, strategic vision, creating an offer, bargaining, and either agreeing or not. Note that an entire chapter on strategies and tactics will follow later in this book. And there is a separate chapter about contracts. The topics of renegotiating and final contract settlement weave through several chapters.

For the moment, let us tie the negotiation process together with what lays the foundation for all else in it: due diligence, also known as doing your homework. Every real estate negotiation I took part in over the past twenty years draws on this first step. Think of due diligence as the component of the real estate negotiation process that is always present, whether in the initial planning, which strategy and tactics to use, in creating and presenting an offer, or in the back and forth between the parties.

One little detail not yet known or found out about at the beginning of the process might show up later and change the entire negotiation and its outcome. Focus and attention to detail help you navigate this terrain. Due diligence, though a definite big preparatory step therefore is also a fluid component in any negotiation.

Here is a quick example. A seller I represented disclosed everything she remembered and found in her records about the home. She agreed to complete a full inspection, which takes away negotiating power from the buyer. She arranged a professional deep cleaning and even baked cookies for the first open house. Although we delivered the home vacant at close of escrow, she moved out only a week before the closing. Lo-and-behold, an unsightly stain from a large plant she once owned appeared on the otherwise pristine hardwood floor in her living room when the movers rolled up the carpet.

After some discussion about how to address the issue, we agreed that I would call the buyer's agent and offer a fixed dollar amount to the buyer. The buyer's response was less than gracious. He accused us of having lied and wanted a significant reduction in the price.

After several days of going back and forth, he finally agreed to the amount we originally offered him. That one little detail brought plenty of stress into our lives literally just before closing the transaction. My seller learned several though lessons, one of them being "disclose everything," and that "greedy buyers can easily turn aggressive." She also learned that having a Plan B until the closing papers are complete and signed and the transaction is final is mandatory.

Cover your bases by taking due diligence seriously and remembering that everything is negotiable. The party best prepared can plan better, assess the other party and the property better, and often gains leverage and power.

Besides, to negotiate well, it is as important to know the true property value as it is to ferret out the other party's motivation. Once the parties know the facts, they can ask for what they want without taking advantage of or cheating others. Fairness in negotiations bears many fruits down the line, including repeat business and a stellar reputation.

Here then is a more in-depth breakdown of real estate negotiation steps.

- Engage appropriate professionals.
    - Find them by referral.
    - Interview them.

- o Ask questions.

- o What do you appreciate about them?

  - Honesty.

  - Integrity.

  - Professionalism.

  - Responsiveness.

  - Communication style.

- Preliminary homework.

  - o Needs and wants assessment.

  - o Gain clarity about what is acceptable and what is not.

  - o This allows you effectively to communicate your expectations and boundaries.

  - o Market analysis.

  - o Financial set-up and readiness.

  - o Timeline decisions.

- Identifying the property.

- More homework.

- Disclosures.

- Property and market-specific analyses.

- Use market value versus asking price as your starting point.

- Market time.

- Average market time for similar homes.

- Average market time in the market.

- Comparables (Comps).

- Know what else is on the market.

- Square footage.

- Room counts.

- Taxes.

- Homeowner association fees.

- Zoning.

- Illegal additions.

- Neighborhood.

- The "why"

  o Is it a seller's or a buyer's market?

  o How do you propose to add value to the negotiation?

  o How will you identify mutual interests between the parties?

  o What competition might you expect?

  o Assessment of the parties.

  o How motivated is the seller?

  o How motivated is the buyer?

  o Decide on the offer price.

  o Will bidding be possible?

  o Is this a starting offer?

  o If so, what is the highest amount the buyer will pay?

    ▪ In what increments?

    ▪ Is this the highest offer amount?

- Is it a lowball offer?

- Write and present the initial offer.

  o Show the seller that your offer is in their best interest.

  o Justify your position.

  o Show the other party your level of commitment to the deal.

- Await the response.

  o Is the seller countering?

  o Is the buyer countering?

  o Are back up offers a possibility?

  o Know when to walk away.

- Multiple Offer Situations.

  o Highest and best offers.

  o Contingency period adjustments.

  o What concession could either the buyer or the seller offer?

o   Know when to walk away.

- Offer acceptance or rejection.

Bargaining is part and parcel of the above list. It is integral to negotiating versus a separate component. The previous chapter presented many of these negotiating components more in-depth. And yes, there is much to consider. Negotiating is a multi-faceted discipline that encompasses the psychology of persuasion, planning, strategy, diplomacy (yes, even in real estate), emotional intelligence and business skills. Negotiation is as much about the personalities that negotiate with one another as it is about the object of the negotiation, in this case the property.

Chapter II details the finer points about the parties, the personalities, the interests, and perceptions present in all negotiations. As you already know negotiating parties may be individuals, corporations, banks (REOs), government agencies (HUD) or non-profits. Each entity has a distinct face, and a distinct mindset and approach.

The mindset that drives a negotiating strategy has implications for the language negotiators use. If a party mentions that a certain negotiating point might be acceptable or possible, it might be a tip off that it is receptive to certain proposals, conditions, and terms. Likewise, the party's language may reveal that they want to do business with you. "We look forward to your reply" may communicate this.

The mindset of the parties defines language and leverage. Leverage refers to a negotiating party's advantage, an advantage by which that party may exert power. Positive leverage in real estate negotiations is about creating value for the other party. And creating value is about solving the problems that party has while also solving one's own negotiation-specific problems. In that scenario, the aim is a fair negotiation.

Negative leverage shows distrust in the other party and its intentions. The fear of being taken advantage of and coming up short then leads to manipulation and even to bullying the other party into agreeing to something that may not be in its interest.

A negotiating party's mindset defines negotiations and their outcomes. Pay attention to both and view them in alongside other findings and facts. Yes, this returns us to doing our homework. And finally, trust your intuition. Use it to guide you here.

Next, note that the other party may have other alternatives to doing business with you. Negotiation results then also hinge on what other options your negotiating partners have. This means that negotiation may result in success or failure. There is little in between. But do your best to gain the respect of the other party in either outcome. Doing so opens future doors and the ability to come back to the table and either revive a negotiation or start a new one.

The structure of deal making revolves around creating value for yourself **and** for the other party. Neither allow the other party to take advantage of you, nor take advantage of the other party. Accomplish this by using emotional and social intelligence and by leveraging your strength and your assets. Contrary to popular belief, emotions can be enormously helpful when negotiating because they communicate authenticity, and they engage the other party.

This does not mean that collaboration is always the answer in negotiations. As already mentioned, the classic definition of any negotiation is a meeting of the minds. It is the desire to agree. Yet, that desire does not and cannot guarantee that differences of opinion will not arise.

How to handle those differences and resolve them is therefore of utmost importance and one of the first topics to address when negotiating. Many parties approach others in a collaborative spirit but have never thought about what collaboration looks like. What happens when differences of opinion arise? How will a collaborative approach resolve such differences? What are the available mechanisms? In collaborative negotiations, let the first agreement between the parties be about such a mechanism. This is important because agreeable individuals without a mechanism to resolve differences between themselves will find themselves in negotiations that end before they begin.

Negotiation mindset and strategy set the tone of any negotiation, driven by the "who, the "why," the "what," and "how." Persuasion, influence, logic, emotional engagement, trust, respect, power, bargaining, problem solving, and compromise all expound negotiating. Negotiating then is a core skill fundamental to all we do with other people. Its importance is paramount. It is a skill worth developing.

The multi-dimensionality of negotiations harkens back to one key ingredient that ensures successful negotiations: trust. The reason is that trust between the parties adds value to all parties. Always start with trust and seek to build it. You may think of this as naïve, but it is not when you also verify. Let the mantra "trust and verify" guide your negotiations. Put verification procedures for all facts, figures and claims in place and use them. When you follow this guideline, several other results follow.

One of them is that building trust is a skill that relies on getting out of one's own way. It relies on keen observation, curiosity, insight, intuition, and facts. Yes, I said facts. The principle of "trust and verify" sets a high standard which is not lost on the other party. However, should the other party withhold information from you, the issue usually is lack of respect. Then your job becomes to change the situation. Sometimes a few honest words accomplish this, but what will work clearly relates to when and how the issue started.

Some parties will play dirty tricks, lie, and cheat at every turn. Real estate agents might do this by stirring buyers to a certain home to increase their commission. Buyers, sellers, and investors might do this by putting in contingencies designed to buy them time. Do your homework in all cases and tighten the contingency timelines. If that does not work, end the negotiations. These buyers, sellers and investors are showing you their modus operandi and you will not change it. You may try but do so at your own risk.

Negotiations also invite creativity and power because the better you become at negotiating, the more you realize that money is only one part of negotiating. Granted, it is an impressive one that most people interpret as proof of results, but it is only one result.

When dealing with deadlocks and conflicts, give the other party a way out. One of the best ways to accomplish this is to find an alternative solution. Build on common ground and on questions that identify the other party's interests and needs. Use language the other party would use to help them own the alternative solutions. This can work wonders when a party backs itself into a corner, as with giving ultimatum like "this is my best and final offer" or "take it or leave it."

By the same token, if you are inclined to take the first offer without negotiating it even a little, you may leave money on the table. The situation invites buyer's or seller's remorse, unless you follow all the important negotiation guidelines, and the offer goes through the normal back and forth of the process. It is a psychological fact that if something is too easy to get, questions about having gotten less than you could or should have floats through the mind. Even in multiple offer scenarios, it is advantageous to issue a counteroffer that solicits the "highest and best offer."

This naturally leads us to concessions and their use and value in real estate negotiations. Concessions are benefits, discounts, and add-ons buyers or sellers offer to close a deal. Concession can help seal the deal. If a party wants a concession, it should ask for it because their negotiation counterpart may never offer it otherwise.

When asking for concessions be ready to concede something in return. It is a bit of a tit for tat situation. And start with the concession that is most important to you, then move yourself to the others. It is often best to ask for concessions one by one, unless bundling your concession requests are natural components of the transaction. An example of this would be consolidating all contingency timelines.

Other concessions encompass sellers offering to pay part or all the closing costs, or to add appliances or a home warranty into the mix. For properties that do not have parking, the seller might pay for a stipulated parking fee amount, etc. Some buyers might offer to pay for a portion of the real estate transfer taxes that sellers must pay. Remember, every number in the agreement is negotiable.

Concessions add value and/or dollars to the transaction, and they are particularly powerful in situations where the parties are in rapport. They also set offers apart from other run-of-the-mill offers seller may receive. Concessions create goodwill and they work best if buyers and sellers trade them instead of only one party giving a concession. The best concessions are reciprocal.

Perhaps the seller wants to use the title company he likes and asks the buyer to make that concession. Otherwise, buyers and their agents choose the title company. The buyer could ask for a concession that is equally important to him. That could be many things. Whatever it is, it should be reasonable and in the same value range as the concession the seller makes.

Sometimes sellers ask for a rent back and buyers concede one. However, this is dicey. It is best for the seller to deliver a vacant property to the buyer at close of escrow. That is especially true because rent backs can bring unwelcome surprises, such as the seller wanting more time or making no effort to vacate the property. Some rent back concessions also come at $0 to the seller, a concession that is more common in seller's markets. In that case avoid problems by correctly phrasing the concession.

Buyers and sellers may decide not to make concessions at all. For example, a buyer may have limited liquid funds and therefore may want to take a concession that would increase the earnest money amount off the table. And of course, it is fine to say "no" to a concession request or to reframe and renegotiate it to get a concession that is more valuable to you. Just remember to make it reasonable. You could ask, "is this the best you can do?" and listen to the answer.

Other important facts about negotiating include that negotiating an agreement, a contract, is the lifeblood of real estate transactions. That said, realtors® and brokers cannot dispense legal advice unless they are also JDs. Most of the time, agents and brokers represent the parties versus buyers, sellers and investors representing themselves.

As a quick aside, it has become an almost standard practice for real estate investors to possess a real estate license. So, the brokerage they form then represents them. This makes little sense for small real estate investor who complete only a few transactions. It makes sense for an investor who has volume and scale.

Knowledge of the facts and collection of appropriate external data is paramount in any negotiation. Besides this, knowledge of the best alternatives to a negotiated agreement for either buyer or seller also is a good idea. For instance, there may be a gap between the buyer's and the seller's initial offer. You could close the gap in several ways.

One is by holding your position without budging and hoping the other party has no other offers. Just know that hope is not a strategy. - Another is to let the other party set their number and terms first and letting them wait before countering. Doing this allows assessing the offer and the ability to formulate the best response. Or you could find alternative ways to give the party what they want. Or you could simply accept the other party's demand or offer. Caution: You must understand the consequences of these responses before proceeding.

When you make an offer, attempt to present it face to face when possible. Even if you have an agent representing you, your agent can do so for you. In the negotiations I am party to, I get to know the other party and their intentions and desires, then negotiate from this position. My clients often stand apart just with this approach, often because the other party knows what they are getting and with whom they are dealing. The idea is to perform due diligence in such a way that the other party feels at ease and treated fairly.

In the San Francisco/Bay Area listing agents have specific instructions for accepting offers, mainly due to the long-lasting seller's market. Bay area real estate markets are currently shifting. New practices may result from the shifting markets.

For example, the market remains a red-hot seller's market in some localities in the East Bay, but in San Francisco many more listings are on the market now. While San Francisco is still not a true buyer's market, buyers have much more choice and more leverage than in the past. This dynamic plays out for some properties, yet those which "every buyer wants" remain highly competitive.

Even before COVID-19, agents, brokers, and sellers did not receive offers face-to-face. Of course, the pandemic necessitates electronic submissions. Given this reality, it is hard to overstate the importance of preparation, of professional relationships, and of pro-active real estate professionals.

Although offers are sometimes verbal, most people do not take verbal offers seriously as those indicate interest but not necessarily forthcoming action. All serious offers must be in writing, especially since real estate transactions are multi-faceted and complex.

Focus on the items both sides agree on when negotiating. And get to "no" fast because a "no" allows you to assess the other party, then find agreement from that position. Naturally, you must determine whether there is a way to convert a "no" to a "yes." There are many ways to do this, and sometimes the passage of time is the buyer's or the seller's best friend.

Another way to bring the parties closer to consummating a deal is by appealing to experts and by using documentation to one's advantage. Just be aware that if your initial offer is far apart, nothing at all may happen and the offer may be dead, at least in its initial iteration. If that happens, you can either decide not to pursue the potential deal or write a fresh offer and start over. Read more about these options in the chapter on contracts for different real estate transaction types, how they differ, and the contracts that address them.

Preparation, also known as homework or due diligence, is the most important aspect of any negotiation, especially for novice negotiators. The more you think through what you want, what your opponent wants, and what trades could get you there, the better you can adapt on the fly as additional information comes to light.

It is possible to ignore the importance of doing one's homework, but it is hardly possible to overstate its importance. All negotiations require it and it is indispensable in high-stakes and high dollar contracts, like real estate contracts. The reason for this is that buying or selling real estate carries risks and one of the best ways to mitigate risk is to know the property, the market it is in, its potential liabilities, and its upside potential.

Due diligence, done well, also uncovers opportunities that otherwise might stay hidden. Learning about the property you want to buy, or sell, or invest makes good business sense. It leads to understanding the numbers, the other party's needs, desires, and motivations. This affects your communication throughout the process. You may even discover how to add value to the negotiations or see how to add value to the property once you own it.

Although it sounds as though doing our homework is a task done once, it is in fact a process. Additional facts can emerge. Numbers and circumstances can change. Still, the initial homework sets a baseline. Sellers use it to determine a property's asking price and the right selling strategy.

Buyers and investors use it to arrive at their initial offer for the property. All parties use it to assess where the value lies. Any party may take this one step further and consider the other party's interests before ever meeting them. That is smarter yet.

Extensive research, preparation and planning includes getting and analyzing information about the market, the property, the parties, the desired outcomes, the financing and financing options, improvement potential and so on. To get all this information start by visiting the property, read the disclosures, analyze the market the property is in, analyze the overall market, speak with the other party or their representative, get property inspections, call a real estate attorney for items your agent cannot answer. The list goes on, but I am sure you get the idea.

For example, sellers might consider what kind of buyer they wish to attract. A retail buyer, defined here as someone who wants a turnkey property, has different interests and requirements than a real estate investor. An investor who fixes and flips single-family homes investigates items distinct from those an investor buying apartment buildings or selling office or retail buildings investigates.

For this reason, investigate and understand real estate valuation methodologies. Valuations methods are appraisal methods. All valuations methods contain bias. If you understand their premise, what data they include, their vantage points of the data used, whether they rely on projections, and what properties and property transactions they serve best, you gain an advantage. Although detailing valuation methodologies is beyond this book, the most common methodologies are the sales comparable approach, the cost approach, and the income capitalization approach.

Valuation methodologies rely on quantifiable data. They rely on numbers. Numbers provide buyers, sellers, and investors with market feedback. They are tools in assessing the competitive landscape and market trends and cycles, and in setting realistic expectations and goals. Buyers, sellers, and investors gain a historical perspective of the markets, though they may run projections as part of their analyses. Therefore, property valuations also pinpoint property market value, cashflow (if applicable), and as yet untapped opportunities.

Appraisers are in the business of valuing property, but so are realtors®. The difference is that appraisers possess licenses that stamp their work official. That is true even though appraisers may or may not know the market in which they appraise property. In contrast, realtor® valuations carry the name of Broker Price Opinions (BPOs), and while most realtors® know the market the property is in, their valuation are "opinions" and are therefore unofficial. Either use the same methodologies and banks often get a BPO first, then follow it with an official appraisal once a transaction and its loan moves forward.

Naturally, buyers, sellers and investors could do such property valuations on their own, so long as they access the right data and use the right tools. Therein lies the rub because it may prove difficult to access proprietary MLS data. Sites such as Zillow, Trulia, Realtor.com. supply unreliable data that comes to them from the MLS and that has challenges. Read more about those issues in the first books in this series. That is one more reason most consumers have representation and investors get real estate licenses.

Our primary concern about property valuations here is at arriving at the initial offer, the offer that officially begins a negotiation. Property valuations clearly are important tools for all parties. Investors aim is to make a profit or create cash flow or both. Many investors use their own formulas to arrive at the offer range for a property.

Although they consider MLS data, MLS data is more "retail" driven and shows fair market value, something that is less useful to investors. An investor strategy of "fix and flip," "rehabbing," or "wholesaling" requires other components besides fair market value. Real estate gurus like Ron LeGrand have a brand based on their valuation formulas. Google "maximum allowable offer (MAO)" to find the formula and variations, applications, and opinions about it.

In contrast to investors, retail buyers pay, well, retail. Overall, those buyers are buying for themselves. They want to live in the property. Savvy real estate sellers also aim to sell at retail prices. And property investors aim to buy at a discount and, depending on their strategy, may sell at retail prices or at below market prices that still net them a profit.

In the past several years, the hybrid model of house hacking arrived. It is a model for property buyers who have little cash to their names and who are willing to do put sweat equity into a property to improve it. House hacking strategy is to buy and own a multi-family property in which to live while upgrading and/or renovating the property. The property is their primary residence, and they can afford to buy it because the property needs work and the tenants in the other units of the building pay their mortgage.

Again, the initial offer price depends on many factors, many of which we discussed in this chapter. More approaches and details appear in the next few chapters. Chapter V discusses negotiation strategies and tactics rounds out the negotiation fundamentals chapters, setting the stage for contracts, their meaning, importance, and wealth building effects.

CHAPTER IV

Too many people are thinking of security instead of opportunity. They seem to be more afraid of life than death. — James F. Byrnes

Common Fears and Mistakes

Fear and its impact

Fear is part of the human experience. It is an emotion, albeit a negative one. The precedents to fear are indecision and worry. Of course, the topic of fear fills tomes of books, doctoral theses, newspapers, and clinical reports. You may refer to any of these to gain a good understanding of the subject. Fear appears in human interactions, including in negotiations. In pointing out how fears enter negotiations and what effects they have, you will learn what to look for and how to overcome them.

It hardly comes as a surprise that many great leaders in all fields, including in business and real estate, have fears. They are human beings like the rest of us. What distinguishes them is that they recognize that fears are states of mind. Instead of focusing on the negative state of mind of fear, they focus on positive emotions.

Fear or other negative emotions such as anger, hatred, or jealousy create the same results they communicate. Positive emotions, such as desire, love, and hope, draw in the same energies they send out. Positive emotions balance our lives. It is therefore preferable and beneficial to engage positive emotion. This idea makes sense but putting it in practice is much more difficult. The reason for this is that it is only long-time practice of these emotions that produces such results.

A person's state of mind as expressed by the emotions, becomes an integral part of the person's character. Naturally, this also shows up in real estate negotiations. Therefore, it is worthwhile touching on the subject, its effects, and implications. For any reader wishing to master any fear, study the classic *Think and Grow Rich* by Napoleon Hill or read about outstanding leaders. Histories, memoirs, and biographies are wonderful starting points.

It is wise to know and understand your own fears. It is also wise to know and understand those of the opposing party. If that sounds like a tall order, start with yourself and take an interest in human nature. Strive to overcome your own fears when negotiating. Many of our emotions are subconscious, so doing this takes effort, study, and reflection to master fears.

Emotions of fear of loss, fear of poverty, fear of being disliked rise to the surface in negotiations. These negative emotions lead to making mistakes. Although neither you nor the other party may articulate them, they are palpable. Never underestimate this intangible element in negotiations.

Master negotiators overcome the emotional state of fear by transmuting it into a positive emotional state. Lest you misunderstand my meaning, this does not mean that they walk around waving peace symbols. Nor does it mean that they ignore the facts. Nor that they ignore either the mentality, mindset or approach of the other party.

Master negotiators take all into account. They assess with whom they are dealing. And, having done their homework, they stay calm and seek to find solutions. Yet, they are not pushovers.

Common negotiating fears and mistakes appear here for three reasons: to make you aware of them and help you recognize them, and to overcome them. Only then can you step up, do your part, and improve. You will reap rich rewards for taking on fears. Rewards may include money, the right property for you, better relationships, knowing who you are, and leading life on your terms.

As you can see, this is seldom about beating out the other party. Rather, it is about starting off on the right foot and with the best vantage point. Any negotiator who follows these precepts has an immediate advantage in negotiations, especially if the other party fails to do the same.

Fears about negotiating

- Fear of not being able to negotiate.
  This one takes many forms including

  o Low self-confidence.

  o Not knowing what you bring to the table.

  o Lack of negotiating skills.

  o Not negotiating, e.g., leaving without asking for more.

- o This fear is a variant of the fear of getting something worse.

- o Not being informed about the, etc.

- o Asking unqualified parties for advice.

- o Getting swayed by poor advice.

- o Not understanding the real estate negotiating process.

  - How to buy a property.

  - How to sell a property.

  - Legal real estate requirements.

  - How loans work.

  - The role of the different parties in the transaction.

- Fear of being judged.

  - o How the other party will see you if you ask for too much.

  - o Fear of appearing ignorant.

  - o Fear of being disliked.

- Fear of rejection

  - Inexperience.

  - The other party might walk out.

  - How that party will perceive you.

  - How your team will perceive you.

  - No leverage.

  - The other party seems intimidating because they have more players.

  - The deal seems intimidating because it is large.

- Fear of appearing incompetent.

  - Self-confidence too high or too low.

  - Unnecessarily dragging out negotiations.

  - Sometimes leads to negotiators sharing too much or too little data.

Look out for variations on these themes.

Now, let us move to common negotiating mistakes, some of which result from the fears we just covered.

See the list on the next page.

Negotiating mistakes

- Guessing instead of doing your homework.

  - Homework includes CMAs, checking reports, inspections.

  - Ignorance about other cultures.

  - Ignorance about the other party.

- Relying on opinions of friends, family, acquaintances.

  - Everyone has an opinion.

  - Few are experts.

  - Even fewer understand the potential effect of their opinion.

- Choosing the wrong starting point

  - Too high.

  - Too low.

- The goal is undefined or unknown

  - What are you negotiating for?

- o What are the outcomes you want?

- o You have a timeline, right?

- Cluelessness about negotiating language.

- Lack of alternatives.

  - o No exit strategy in place.

  - o No concession strategy in place.

- Wasting time on unimportant issues.

- Getting stuck on positions.

- Unethical behavior and shortcuts.

  - o Lies.

  - o Threats.

  - o Playing games.

- Ignoring reasonable requests.

  - o Not listening.

- Taking things personally.

- Letting emotions take over.

- Taking advantage of the other party.

- Impatience.

- Failing to make counteroffers.

- Discomfort with silence.

- Attachment to the property (either as a buyer or a seller).

- Going it alone.

  - Trusting no one, including those who represent you.

  - No team in place.

  - An "if you want to do it right, do it yourself" attitude.

Additional real estate specific items that may lead to negotiating mistakes follow. They are:

- Failure to understand the laws, rules, and regulations—local or otherwise—that relate to buying and selling property.

- Not knowing whether the current market environment is a buyers' market or a sellers' market.

- Missing assessment whether the other party has other choices.

- Clueless about current market supply and demand.

    o This also applies to submarkets.

    o In commercial real estate, this becomes even more important than in residential real estate.

- Lack of knowledge about local housing policies and challenges.

- Not investigating what development plans exist for the property's area.

- Not factoring in economic changes, which might affect the property.

- Or any other governmental or local programs that affect real estate?

For example, in San Francisco, the Community Opportunity to Purchase Act (COPA) is in place for multi-unit buildings.

- Failure to investigate new construction that is happening or in the planning stage for the property's neighborhood and market?

  - Luxury condos?

  - Affordable housing?

  - Commercial property?

  - Or something else?

- Ignorance of local news and local trends.

- No knowledge of real estate terms.

- Unclear goals and strategies.

- There is a big difference between planning for retirement, dealing with divorce, job changes, the need to make money right away, and so on.

- Lack of understanding what it means to be a motivated seller or buyer and/or encountering motivated sellers and buyers.

- Ignorance of market metrics.

- Lack of knowledge about tax consequences of selling or buying property

- Mindset assessment issues.

  Do you possess the right attitude, confidence without being cocky, understanding the market value of the property, realistic price expectations etc.?

- Unrealistic pricing.

  - Some sellers set prices based on what they would like to net, and that may or may not be in accordance with the market.

  - Are you basing your pricing and offering on research, or are you shooting from the hip?

- Undefined bottom line.

- Absence of a contingency plan.

- Missing or old in-depth market analysis (CMA) or appraisal.

- A dated property.

  - Does the property need repairs?

- o Does it have curb appeal?

- o How does your home or property compare to others of the same property type?

- o Know the differences and how they affect the property's value and price.

- No inspections.

- Lack of a plan to move. (Applies to properties you live in.)

  - o Are you prepared financially, emotionally, logistically?

- Ignoring emotions are you feeling about the process and how are you dealing with them.

- Underestimating the pressures and demands of selling property.

Outwitting fear

Mistakes and fears pervade real estate negotiations. Statements such as "I dislike negotiating" or "I can't negotiate" are expressions of fear. They are also excuses for speaking without clarity, for failing to stand up, and for incurring losses. They even serve to escape being disliked when making a demand. So how to outwit them?

If you put into perspective what the potential outcome could be and are okay with it, you are on the path to overcoming your fears. However, before discussing ways to help overcome the fear of negotiating, I will say this: sometimes fear is a warning sign that helps avert disaster. Anyone "overcoming" fear with bluster and ego is in for a rude awakening. Neither equal confidence nor courage.

Broaden your view of what is possible. Check and double check your assumptions about receiving what you need and desire. Some negotiations become incongruent when one or both parties feel or decide that they cannot have all they want. Such beliefs change the dynamics between the negotiating parties. A party therefore may believe they cannot ask for what they want and that they must be reasonable. This leads them to compromise too early, in the process leaving things on the table.

All parties can make mistakes in negotiations. Many do. Remember that it is not whether people make mistakes because they will, but instead how they handle these mistakes and correct them. That said, there is an entire spectrum of mistakes. It is easy to rectify some mistakes, while others can sink the entire negotiation. In other words, some mistakes are disastrous, others are not.

Real estate negotiations are big dollar negotiations and money is a symbolic medium. Money, or rather what money means to you or someone else, elicits emotions, expectations, desires, needs, and dynamics. Emotions, in turn, expose personality traits. This is true in all negotiations. For this reason alone, it is a good idea to engage professionals in handling and guiding negotiations.

Negotiations can also intimidate, especially given that both parties want to get the best deal. In real estate, the parties often assume that only one of them can win. That means the parties pit themselves against one another from the start and declare war on one another.

Yet, skilled negotiators can work under the many pressures that negotiations present. Some realtors® and attorneys are worth their weight in gold. Their guidance is indispensable in correct property pricing or in getting the most out of the deal. Or in securing other concessions. Or in communicating for and with the parties. Or in completing all due diligence. Or in writing the contract. Or in staying neutral.

However, be the best negotiator you can be.

All masters start at the same place. There are no shortcuts. Improve your skills at every opportunity. Use detailed preparation and planning. They build confidence, an important ingredient in overcoming fears about negotiating and an equally important one in reaching successful agreements. - The next chapter on strategies and tactics will set you on course to hone your skills.

Watch for our upcoming course on real estate investing.

Get the course announcement when it's ready.

Please sign up for the mailing list here

www.realestate-negotiation.com .

Get this *BONUS when you sign up:*

My negotiation with the tailor in Nepal.

The promise:

Occasional announcements only.

No other marketing emails will arrive.

And you can unsubscribe at any time.

CHAPTER V

Strategy without tactics is the slowest route to victory.
Tactics without strategy is the noise before defeat. —
Sun Tzu

Strategies and Tactics

We have covered a lot of ground up to this point. I imagine that some of you skipped to this section before reading the rest of the book. That is okay, but the important concepts and concrete action steps in this chapter require integration. You must read the other chapters to put it all together.

We will start with a bit of instructive fun—with the story of Cleopatra (69—30 B.C.), the Macedonian Greek who ruled Egypt.

Huh?

Hold tight if the sultry image of Elizabeth Taylor just flickered across the screen of your mind. Modern day images and portray Cleopatra as a seductress, as an icon for makeup and fashion. That image is mostly invented. Cleopatra was an exquisite strategist and negotiator. She possessed an incredible intellect, wit, charm, wealth, and what we would call business acumen today.

Cleopatra aligned herself with the two most powerful men of her time, one became her lover, the other one her husband. She saved her kingdom from falling to the Romans and amassed an empire. Her life dramatically ended in suicide to spare herself from having lost it all.

She was controversial in her time and in all other times. This short vignette only covers the most pertinent lessons for negotiating. The first one is that Cleopatra realized the necessity of knowing the other party. Her skillful communications and her courage enticed both Julius Caesar and Mark Anthony to do her bidding. She advanced the interests of her empire and her own interests throughout her 22-year reign.

Cleopatra could do this because of her skills, her vision, strategy and tactics. Cleopatra built strategic alliances. She did this through influence, power, public relations, and strategic communication. Strategic alliances comprised her core strategy, her negotiation signature. She used varied tactics to fulfill it. - All effective negotiators rely on alignment of strategy and tactics. So does anyone negotiating real estate.

Strategies and tactics belong together. They depend on one another. A strategy without tactics is unfulfillable. In that case, the strategy remains a pipe dream. Conversely, tactics without strategy miss the aim. This is akin to archers using their bow and arrows to hit everything but the scoring ring.

Strategy defines long-term goals and the plan to achieve these goals. Tactics list specific actions and resources they require to support and achieve strategic goals. This means strategy and tactics must align and work together, but they are not the same.

Resources may limit strategies, as in a real estate investor who wants to own, say, ten commercial properties but has funds only for one. That investor might use resources in creative ways. The investor might also factor in time to reach the goal and start with one property, then add others.

Our investor's initial strategy might shift over time. The investor might leverage what he has, thereby speeding up the growth of the property portfolio. Strategy reviews are mandatory to do this well and to adapt to changes and circumstances.

Excellent strategies rely on meticulous research. Brilliant strategies also require reflection on the goal, on one's personal proclivities, and on one's team's abilities and personalities. Long-term vision as defined by the strategy is only possible through such inquiries and activities.

All real estate buyers, sellers and investors must have an initial strategy and a plan. They must know their target market, know the numbers, and their action steps. In addition, the initial strategy must include an exit strategy. All these components set them apart.

- Negotiate after preparing to the nth degree.

- Drive negotiations through information and knowledge.

- Commit to lifelong learning.

- Plan everything.

A quick word about exit strategies. Exit strategies are plans which specify ways to deal with unforeseen circumstances. Although these circumstances are unknown and may never happen, buyers, sellers and investors must consider them. For example, how would you pay the mortgage if you lost your job? Or how would you address sudden vacancies in your properties? Are you banking on appreciation to net a profit?

During the Great Recession from 2007 to 2009, many sellers and investors who bought property in the boom years either lost money or lost property to foreclosure. They had no exit strategies. The Great Recession and these enormous losses had ripple effects for years afterwards. The current pandemic might effect similar dynamics. That is because the U.S. economy is at a low, unemployment at record highs, rents are down, and property value are adjusting. Exit strategies are as important as ever.

You get the idea. Considering these possibilities ahead of time helps you make better plans and fulfill your strategy or adjust it. Exit strategies mitigate risk and offer flexibility in different market environments. Here are some real estate exit strategies:

- Wholesaling

- Seller financing

- Lease options

- Buy and hold

- Refinancing

- Rehabbing

- Flipping

- Property appreciation

- House hacking

- And many more

All these strategies can generate profits. All of them could also be your initial strategy. Consider them and select two or three as back-ups.

After this little digression, we now return to negotiation strategies. What you read below are negotiation styles and negotiation strategies. They are integral to one another.

- Collaborative negotiations (win-win)

  - Build strategic alliances.

  - Create and add value.

- Seek to understand but know your value proposition and needs.

- Seek mutual gain.

- Accommodating negotiations (I lose, you win)

  - Friendly.

  - Relationship oriented.

  - Want to create a positive dynamic.

- Competitive or zero-sum negotiations (I win, you lose)

  - Looking out for number one.

  - Ignores the other party's needs.

  - Often based on power and leverage.

  - Gains are at the other party's expense.

  - Focused and results driven.

  - Sometimes aggressive.

- Seeking compromise (we both win some and lose some)

  - Fairness driven.

- o Settling for less.

- Avoidance negotiations (lose-lose).
  - o Dislike conflict.
  - o May evade negotiations altogether.
  - o Passing the negotiation to another member of their team.

All these negotiation styles are distinct, and they use different strategies. They often result in different outcomes. The parties might become more and more antagonistic, as is often the case in competitive negotiations. Or the parties might seek compromise. Or they might avoid conflicts altogether but watch out, aggression may take over when avoidance is present. In the latter case, negotiations can end with escalating conflicts. Neither party backs down when conflicts escalate. And that situation takes expertise to defuse.

Negotiations range from being easy to difficult to seemingly impossible. If a party feels taken advantage of, they either walk away or make implementation painful. Most want fair treatment. They want to get or pay a fair price. All want to get value.

Although the concept of fairness is subjective and overused, it remains important in negotiations. Understanding what fairness means to the other party is part of your homework.

The idea of fairness shows up right away in real estate negotiations. Sellers want a fair price, usually market value. And fair market value has nothing to do with what they paid for their homes or properties forty years ago.

And property buyers want to pay a fair price, which usually means the market value of the property. They dislike overbidding or paying more than market value. In fact, most buyers aim to purchase properties slightly below market.

I am purposefully leaving out those buyers who believe that they ought to get a market value property for a fraction of what it is worth. While that sounds wonderful, it is unrealistic. Such buyers often waste much time, energy, and effort on this dream.

Finally, some property investors seek to pay a fair price for the promise of future income. And other property investors want to pay below market prices to factor in improving properties. That may mean they invest in rehabbing or renovating properties, often also known as fix and flip. They could also rezone and or develop the property. Or they might upgrade it for greater income potential. Variations on the theme are manifold. However, the salient feature of property investing is to generate profits.

The above strategies must also consider other factors. Such factors extend to whether the negotiation partners have history. They may have reached agreements in the past. They may even consider future negotiations together. Any long-term association between the parties influences the negotiation options, communications, and results.

Other influencing factors might concern timing and reconsideration of timelines. They might also extend to what items and processes come first and last in the agreement. Such factors and changes demand forethought, strategic deliberation, and approaching the negotiation from a unique vantage point. They make most sense in large, complex deals. The same applies to re-thinking leverage.

Institutional real estate investors, for example, may well use this approach to refine their strategy. Yet, strategy refinements may also benefit run-of-the-mill real estate buyers and sellers and smaller scale real estate investors. They sometimes make a vast difference in the negotiation.

The takeaway is this: Know your negotiation style. Know the other party's negotiation style. Study yourself and the other party before entering a negotiation. The truth of this statement applies to real estate negotiations and negotiations in other fields.

One masterful negotiator comes to mind. It is Nelson Mandela, the anti-apartheid revolutionary and political leader and former president of South Africa. He understood and lived the truths of these statements. His negotiation style was pragmatic and strategic. He was patient and persistent, yet when he made concessions, he never conceded what was most important to him. Perhaps his long incarceration taught him those skills, or it brought out those attributes in his character. No matter, his strategy, style, and tactics averted civil war and bloodshed in South Africa.

Without a doubt, these attributes are as valuable in real estate negotiations as they were to Mandela and the fate of South Africa. That is so, even if real estate negotiation does not decide the fate of a country.

Strategic planning must be thorough to select the right tactics. Mandela masterfully blended strategy and tactics. His strategy was solid, and his tactics allowed him to execute it. You can do the same. The next section then details some important negotiation tactics.

Negotiation Tactics

Strategy and tactics allow negotiators to pursue their aim. A strategy's success may lead to revising that strategy or to implement a different one. Negotiation tactics, however, depend on one's strategy. Tactics align with whichever strategy is in place. They are much easier to adjust than one's strategy because tactics comprise short-term actions. They aim to meet the specific objectives of a strategic plan.

For example, timelines and deadlines are tactics. Assessing any resources, whether time, money, knowledge, or a team, is part of tactical planning. The actions (tactics) you take depend on all these components. Miss one of them and your entire strategy is at risk. The liquidated damages story earlier in this book is a case in point.

Tactics have an obvious purpose. Ideally, they are measurable. Better yet, they can turn negotiations to a party's advantage. From the hundreds of tactics that exist, find those pertinent to real estate negotiations. Consult the list that follows. Be creative. Many tactical variations exist. Just make sure they line up with your strategy.

55 Negotiation Tactics

1. Questions
   a. Ask an open-ended question.
   b. Ask a close-ended question.
   c. Deflect an answer with a great question.
2. Establish rapport.
   a. Smile.
   b. Engage the other party.
   c. Seek to understand before being understood.
   d. Know the other party.
3. Stall for concessions.
4. Concede small.
   a. Concessions can be one-sided or mutual.
   b. Something that sweetens the deal.
   c. Start with the concession most important to you.
   d. Some concessions may equal loss to you but may be worth it in an accompanying "lose the battle, win the war" mindset.
5. *I'll meet you in the middle.*
   a. Also known as "split-the-difference."
   b. Appears to be a fair result when in fact it is to the advantage of the other party.

6. Silence.
    a. It is golden in negotiations.
    b. When confronted by the other party using silence, restate your offer.
7. Is that your best offer?
    a. *You've got to be kidding.*
    b. This tactic elevates their offer as the new starting point.
8. The ultimatum.
    a. Take it or leave it.
    b. The offer disappears at a specific time.
9. *You'll be sorry.*
    a. Ambush. Attack.
    b. Threats.
10. Bluffing
    a. Pretending to agree to something you have no intention of doing.
    b. Pretending to have more money, connections, resources than one has.
    c. Call the other party's bluff as soon as possible.
11. Concealing one's intentions
    a. Keeps one's intentions hidden.
    b. A hidden agenda.

    c. Intentionally leading the other party down the wrong path.

    d. Throws the other party off balance.

    e. Disables the other party from defending itself.

12. Lies.

    a. Lacks good faith.

    b. Engenders distrust, resistance, and resentment.

    c. Send the message that this party has no intention for fair dealings.

    d. Puts the other party on the defensive.

13. A nibble

    a. A minor concession.

    b. Often used at the end of a real estate negotiation.

    c. In case of a nibble, the expectation is for the other party to do the same.

14. Say no and stick to it.

    a. No backpedaling allowed.

    b. Any party which backpedals after saying *no* loses the negotiation.

15. Reference an expert opinion.

    a. Experts germane to the negotiation.

b. Research.

c. Books, reports, etc.

d. Facts, statistics, numbers.

16. High authority.

a. Consulting someone in a higher position to get the go ahead.

b. A tactic often in place at car dealerships.

17. Put it in writing.

a. Clarifies positions.

b. Avoids misunderstandings.

c. Makes it official.

d. Enforceable.

18. Uncover the real reason.

a. What does the other party need?

b. What does it want?

c. Moves through the smokescreens.

19. Clarify the ground rules.

a. Avoids misunderstandings.

b. Sets parameters and boundaries.

c. Establishes a process.

20. Isolate agreement.

a. Put the toughest issue last.

b. Sets the tone for a negotiation.

21. If you were in my shoes.

    a. Asking for mercy.

    b. Asking for understanding and consideration.

22. Deflect anger.

    a. Ask for forgiveness.

23. Interruptions

    a. Take negotiations off track.

    b. If interruptions repeat, stop the negotiation.

24. Cherry picking

    a. Selecting parts of the offer one likes and rejecting the others.

25. If X, then Y.

    a. What happens if the other party does not deliver?

    b. What happens if you do not deliver?

26. Good Cop/Bad Cop scenario.

    a. An authority figure who can accept or reject terms.

    b. Either can be real or imagined.

    c. Similar to bringing in the experts.

27. Haggling

    a. Also known as bargaining.

    b. Get more and give less approach.

    c. No concern for the other side or the relationship.

28. Repeat your point of view.

    a. Sound like a broken record.

    b. Can break down the other party and move them in your direction.

29. Launch a tangent.

    a. Introduces additional parts into the discussion.

    b. Diverts from the negotiation.

    c. Can buy time.

    d. Caution! This tactic can backfire.

30. Buy time.

    a. *I'll get back with you about this.*

31. Appeal to fairness.

    a. Establish a fair starting point.

    b. Communicate your belief that the other party is fair in its dealings.

32. Explore options.

    a. What other options achieve the desired results?

33. Move the deadline.

34. Induce guilt.

a. When you feel hurt or betrayed.

35. Find an umpire.

    a. Engage a fair mediator.

36. Persist.

    a. Do not give up.

    b. Develop patience.

37. Dealing with ego.

    a. Massage it.

    b. Know the person you are negotiating with.

    c. Flatter the person.

    d. Sweettalk them.

    e. Shares the pros and the cons. - Known as the Franklin close.

38. Play good guy/bad guy.

    a. Also see Good Cop/Bad Cop.

    b. Pitting conflicting opinions against one another.

39. These boots were made for walking.

    a. Threatens the other party.

    b. Mean it, otherwise you will lose.

    c. If you walk out, the negotiation is dead.

40. The conditional *no*

    a. Says no to the other party.

   b. Leaves the door open to come back to the table.

   c. *At this point it's going to be a no but...*

41. *I do not care about you.*

   a. Sets the tone for a competitive negotiation.

   b. Engenders distrust.

42. *Give it to me straight.*

   a. Builds a bridge.

   b. Establishes honesty.

   c. Preempts other tactics to conceal information or to mislead.

43. *The ball is in your court.*

   a. Signals everything you will offer is on the table.

   b. Awaits a move.

44. *Help me understand.*

   a. Asking for their rationale.

   b. Asking for details.

45. Take time out.

   a. Take a short break.

   b. Cools off emotions.

   c. Resets the discussion.

46. *We have never done that before!*

a. Signals something outside the other party's experience and comfort zone.

b. Refers to standard practice or policy as the basis of the negotiation.

c. Inclines toward no.

47. Highball it.

a. Starts with a significantly higher offer than the starting price.

b. Most often happen is strong seller's markets.

c. If the offering party needs a loan, a high ball offer may not be able to deliver.

48. Lowball it.

a. Starts with a significantly lower offer than the asking price.

b. In many markets, lowball offers stand no chance.

c. Takes advantage of the other party.

d. All about getting what you want, no matter what.

49. *The choice is yours.*

a. Ask the other party to decide.

b. Best when there are several options to choose from.

    c. Usually 3 options to choose from for the other party.

50. Never say yes to the first offer.
    a. Engages the parties.
    b. Makes them feel there is more to consider.
    c. Do this, no matter what the offer.
    d. Helps avert buyer's or seller's remorse.

51. Time is slipping.
    a. Make the other party aware of impending timelines and deadlines.
    b. Let them know you expect them to meet those.

52. *You go first.*
    a. The other party speaks first.
    b. Helps you in answering their demands.
    c. Can establish rapport.

53. Trial balloon
    a. Questions aimed at discerning the other party's position.
    b. Includes what price the other party would accept.

54. Stonewalling
    a. Showing the other party that you are not open to new solutions.
    b. Unresponsiveness.
    c. Or by using language which communicates this.

All those tactics can be effective with the right strategy. You probably realize that some tactics work best with certain strategies, while they will not work with others. Strategies and tactics represent the method to start and complete negotiations. The tactics list is not exhaustive, so investigate further once your strategy is in place.

Remember to lay the right foundations by providing value and adding it. Corollary to the value maxim, strive for fairness in negotiations. If you encounter a party wishing to ignore or circumvent either, run. Refrain from doing business with them unless you wish to invite aggravation. If you are that party, ask yourself why. Assess whether there are better ways to continue.

No matter what you do, start all your negotiations with the end in mind. Nothing eclipses preparation. Conflict resolution in negotiation is a practice. Justify your position, put yourself in the other party's shoes, keep your emotions in check, and know when to walk away.

Although a rejected offer seems to imply failure, it sometimes is the perfect solution to a negotiation. If a buyer or seller rejects an offer, move on. Alternatively, you could explore other options, maybe even with the same party, or you could submit a fresh offer. Move ahead no matter what happens. Dejection has no place in real estate negotiations.

You can always take temporary breaks to recharge your batteries, to assimilate your experience, and to reassess your strategy and tactics. Your negotiations will be better for it. If your negotiation was successful and you now own more property or sold properties you wanted to sell, focus on your next goal. Set its strategy and tactics and refine your skills. It is rare that a party starting out in buying or selling real estate or in real estate investing gets rich with one transaction.

To re-iterate, the negotiation process carries is replete with strategies and tactics. They are essential components of it. Leonardo da Vinci (1483- 1519) embodied this process. I have no idea whether he bought or sold any real estate properties, but he put it like this:

It had long come to my attention that people of accomplishment rarely sat back and let things happen to them. They went out and happened to things.

When you follow this advice, you will experience what I call the wealth effect, which real estate contracts create. And contracts are the next chapter's topic.

CHAPTER VI

Verbal contracts are about as useful as a fart on a treadmill. — Robert Rinder

Contracts

Successful negotiations culminate in contracts. Verbal contracts exist, but they are difficult to prove and to enforce. In verbal contracts it is one person's word against another's, something which engenders miscommunication. Often the parties also believe that they agreed on something, only to find out later that they heard different things. The point of this is to memorialize agreements in writing. Take no chances!

All contracts contain the following essentials:

- Earnest money (initial deposit)
- Financing
  - Cash

- o Loan
- o 1031 Exchange
- o Seller financing
- o Funds via crowdfunding
- Contingencies
  - o Inspections
  - o Finance
  - o Subject to selling another property
  - o Subject to partner approval
  - o ... And others
- Terms
  - o Real estate terms abound but common ones include: days on market (DOM), backup offer, rent back, As-Is, CC&Rs (HOA documents), equity, loan type, escrow holder, pre-approval, proof of funds, preliminary title report, probate, trust sale, REO (foreclosure), short sale, Tenancy-In-Common (TIC)
- Timelines
- Closing date

In addition, some contracts have escalation clauses, which are clauses that can help offers rise to the top in a sea of other offers. Escalation clauses appear in a contract's addendum which says that Mr. or Mrs. Buyer will pay a certain amount more than the highest offer received. That sounds simple enough, but escalation clauses must consider many details, such as the top price the buyer is willing to pay.

Many sellers also will not accept escalation clauses because it is often easier for them to issue a counteroffer that says to submit the "highest and best offer" from all buyers. Sellers also want buyers to offer their highest and best offer first versus playing the "my-offer-can-change-for-the-better" game. Still, in some situations and market environments, the buyer may gain an advantage by adding an escalation clause.

Offers usually arrive in the form of a written real estate contract, signed by the party submitting the offer. Most offers have expiration dates and the other party either accepts the offer, makes a counteroffer, rejects it, or lets it expire without responding.

Let us assume the other party accepts the offer and signs it. Once legal signatures are affixed, either wet signatures or valid digital signatures, the contract becomes enforceable. The legal definition of parties able to enter a contract includes mental capability and adulthood. Minors also cannot enter contracts. Contracts are valid and enforceable only if the parties fulfill these requirements. Contracts that do not fulfill them are non-enforceable, void, or voidable. Parties also cannot enter contracts with illegal aims.

Parenthetically, the power of contracts arose from people beating each other out without regard for others. This often resulted in taking advantage of weaker parties, cheating them and stealing from them. Contracts make this much harder to do, though the possibility lingers. That is why the information you read in chapters II and III is invaluable. But let us return to our discussion.

In case of a counteroffer, the original offer is no longer legally binding. The parties did not agree to the terms. In case the seller rejects the offer, it terminates. Or, if there is no response to the counteroffer, it automatically expires on a specified date and at a specified time stated in the contract. Most real estate contracts contain an expiration date. Otherwise, the negotiating parties would sit in limbo and risk that the contract could suddenly become valid, say, a year after submitting it.

All contracts contain consideration. Consideration constitutes something of value exchanged for the property or services specified in the contract. In most cases consideration is money, though it could also be another property, or something else. Whatever it is, it must have value.

In the real estate business, different contracts serve different functions. Even though this is the case, you could grab a piece of paper and write an offer on it, then present it to the other party. If it contains the elements that make a contract and the other party signs it, you have a contract. Before I elaborate about why this simple practice of creating a contact is unwise, here are the most common types of real estate contracts.

The listing agreement is a contract between property sellers and their representatives, most often real estate agents. Listing agreements vary. They are exclusive agency, exclusive right to sell, or open listing agreements. The most prevalent of them is the exclusive-right-to-sell listing through which the broker receives a commission no matter who sells the property. The other two listing agreement types often mean that the broker may or may not get compensation for any work done on the seller's behalf.

One of the most important components of a listing agreement is the price for which the seller agrees to list the property. While there are other terms and conditions listing agreements cover, those governing the seller/real estate professional relationship, the list price is the springboard that generates buyer interest and offers. The listing agreement with its – hopefully - market-vetted price therefore has implications for any negotiations that follow.

I mention listing agreements here because they are real estate contracts, albeit ones most people only think about if they are property sellers. Buyer agreements also exist, and some agents use them. However, most buyers have no interest in signing such an agreement. They do not want to be beholden to one agent, especially when most of them have little idea how to tell agents apart. That is another subject, one that I discuss in my first two books.

Now, here are the contracts most people are aware of as real estate-specific contracts. They are real estate purchase agreements, contracts that identify property buyers and property sellers. These contracts are sales contracts which specify a particular property. They include the property's legal description and the deed exchanged.

The purchase agreement also specifies the property's price, terms, including the terms of possession, conditions, financial arrangements, earnest money, the closing date and costs, and which items are included or excluded from the sale. It contains important contractual details, obligations, and rights. The purchase contract becomes legally binding once both parties sign it, and the contractual clock runs the moment it becomes binding.

As a quick note, both addenda and amendments may change contractual terms and conditions if both parties agree to them. Addenda often are informational and explanatory. They might cover terms the contract lacks or clarify contract explanations and terms. Amendments, on the other hand, modify terms and conditions of an already accepted contract. Addenda may be attached to the contract or become part of it, while amendments become part of the contract.

Purchase contracts vary. Therefore, review, understand and vet whichever purchase contract you use. Not all contracts are created equal, so you must understand their differences. Seek professionals to help you do so. Do not skip this step.

Then stick with the one you choose for all your transactions for properties you are buying or selling. That means, if you buy or sell single-family homes or condos use a purchase contract specific to those property types. If you buy an office or retail building or land, use a commercial purchase agreement. Use a lease agreement for property leases. I will address leases in short order.

Note that mobile homes are personal property in most states, not real property, unless the land they sit on is part of buying or selling the mobile home. Buying and selling them requires a different purchase agreement for this reason. You may find those applicable to your state on state or county websites. This book contains no further information about mobile home purchases and sales.

The real estate contract you use depends on whether you are buying property with representation, such as a real estate professional or an attorney, or without representation. In the first scenario, your representative is a professional with access to state-specific purchase agreements or local real estate association purchase agreements. The professional will use one of these purchase agreements and insist on using this contract because all other real estate professionals know, use and accept it.

In the second scenario, the one without representation, you will use a general real estate purchase agreement. These purchase agreements often are shorter version of the state or association purchase agreements. They are generic and may or may not address specific legal issues that relate to property acquisitions or sales. You could hire an attorney to vet them for you, but that costs time and money. Instead of doing so, you are likely better off engaging a knowledgeable real estate professional who has access to these documents and can explain them as part of their services.

Real estate purchase contracts serve for various strategies. One difference presents itself when assigning a contract. Most real estate association purchase contracts discourage assignments. One reason is that these contracts are tailored to purchases that involve loans or are all-cash. Lenders shun assignments because they represent higher risk.

However, real estate contract assignments are strategies many real estate gurus advocate because many of their students have little or nothing to their name. They may well work if the guru mentors the person how to use them. However, I believe that it takes a party experienced in assignments to implement them well. They present opportunities and pitfalls. Take this as a word of caution to stay away from them unless you receive such mentorship or are already proficient in executing them.

What assignments mean is a for a contract that you, your real estate professional representative, or your attorney negotiated, and in which the seller agrees to sell the rights to purchase the property to a third party. That third party most often is an investor. Assignments are contracts. Both parties bind themselves to the arrangement. Note that the assignment gives the third party the rights to purchase the property. They do not buy the property and hold no title to the property. Instead, they assign their rights to the property to another buyer and collect an assignment fee from that buyer. Contract assignments stay off the title chain.

Our discussion would hardly be complete without the mention of lease agreements. Lease agreements cover rental fees, terms, and conditions for properties which owners rent out either to residential or to commercial tenants. They considerably vary. They also affect other contracts, such as commercial purchase agreements. There they make big differences in commercial property values and in potential for the property. Lease agreements contain important details about the property and its profitability.

Lease agreements can be short-term or long-term arrangements. They may be for small lessees or for corporate leases. They also range in what they offer those tenants. Residential leases are straightforward, while business and corporate leases can be complex. The latter usually takes much longer to negotiate.

The three main commercial lease types are gross leases, also known as full-service leases, net leases and triple net leases (NNN). Other variations model themselves on these lease types. Tenants pay base rent in a full-service lease, while the landlord covers all other expenses. Those expenses include taxes, maintenance, insurance, and other building expenses. For net leases tenants cover some other expenses besides the base rent. For triple net lease tenants cover the base rent, which usually is lower than in the other lease types, and all other expenses. Retail property leases can also be percentage leases where tenants pay a base rent besides a percentage based on their sales.

The question about price and terms in a contract is always present. Which is better? Price or terms? Property buyers, sellers and investors frequently focus on price and sometimes ignore terms to their detriment. Just as shoppers for a loan often focus on the rate without considering the other variables of the loan, property buyers and sellers gravitate toward the price.

However, terms can make an enormous difference in a real estate negotiation and its resulting contract. A quick example is a buyer who makes an offer contingent on selling a property. That buyer is at a disadvantage and may not get the offer accepted, even if the price exceeds the seller's expectations.

Okay, we have covered some contract basics. One more important point to share about contracts is that there is a whole industry that specializes in contracts: the legal industry. And when dealing with an industry, be aware that arriving at writing and executing contracts is more complex and difficult than it appears. This means working with the right professionals to cover your bases is a good practice.

As an aside, most buyers and sellers are perfectly fine with standardized contracts so long as their real estate professional or attorney can explain the finer points. As you already know, real estate professionals cannot dispense legal advice, unless they are attorneys. That means they are walking a tightrope, and should you have questions or concerns about finer points or laws, codes, regulations, etc., you must seek an attorney. Any excellent real estate professional will tell you so.

In my experience, the only buyers, sellers, and investors who want to debate and alter standardized real estate agreements are attorneys. Sometimes deeper knowledge of the law is a hindrance. However, most savvy attorneys understand that their real estate attorney colleagues wrote the standardized contract. They know that legal precedents are the basis for those contracts. They also understand that they would lose time and money in rewriting the standardized contract and that the other party may not accept their version.

In all my years in real estate, only a few attorneys wanted to debate and rewrite the standardized real estate contract. They usually either disappeared or came around to appreciating standardized contracts. The beauty of the standardized contracts that state or local real estate associations publish is that they are vetted.

Resolved real estate litigations on various real estate issues inform real estate association contracts. That means they are specific to either the state or the county or even the municipality they serve. For instance, members of the San

Francisco Association of Realtors® (SFAR) can avail themselves of the SFAR contracts. And the California Association of Realtors® (CAR) publish a library of real estate-related documents, including contracts their members can use.

Real estate association purchase agreements or contracts written by attorneys address what happens in case a party breaches the contract. They detail available remedies. Further, they consider options to address differences of opinion, factual discrepancies, disputes, and the like. Contractual parties can select arbitration or mediation options, but they must be selected at the start. Parties cannot change them once selected.

Arbitration and mediation offer two different options with big legal ramifications. Real estate professionals can only bring the options to their client's attention. They cannot tell the client which one to choose, nor provide other explanations that could imply giving legal advice. Even if the realtor® is adept in the concepts and their implications, recommending either option is a no, no. Only attorneys can provide this counsel to buyers, sellers or investors.

In case a buyer, seller or investor has no professional representation, the internet offers variations on real estate contracts that lack the official vetting and support of real estate associations. Use them at your own risk. Better yet, engage a real estate attorney to assess how solid they are and whether they will serve you well. Naturally, this takes time and money.

The fine print distinguishes contracts. Read it!

It matters. Even standardized contracts are alterable. That is why reading the contract before signing it pays in spades. Never sign a contract on a whim. Review it thoroughly. Make counteroffers that supersede the items they address once signed by both parties or propose an addendum. When using counteroffers or addenda you are in effect negotiating the contract. Familiarize yourself with the tools at your disposal and use them to best advantage.

In case this is a little too dry and technical for you, here is a Charisma Carpenter quote to lighten it up a bit:

I had been warned not to get on a motorcycle, sort of. I think there is a clause in most general basic contracts to keep yourself in one piece and not alter your looks without telling them first.

Real estate contracts are complex because of the many details that go into them. They capture the pertinent agreement points of the negotiation—in writing. That alone lends them value. Anyone with a deeper understanding of how real estate contracts work will see that money is only one result of a successful agreement. The agreement itself is valuable. Once understood and appreciated, it is duplicatable, allows for creative thinking and application and for solving problems. Without a doubt, contracts create wealth. Learn all you can about them and cultivate relationships with people who can help you do so.

CHAPTER VII

Negotiation Checklist

The noblest pleasure is the joy of understanding.
- Leonardo da Vinci

Great negotiations require meticulous preparation and planning, then engagement, communication, using the tools at your disposal, and reaching agreement. Keep this checklist handy to help you navigate the process.

1. Start with the end in mind and articulate the outcome you want.

    ➢ Your best outcome.

    ➢ Your plan B.

    ➢ What happens if agreement is not possible?

        ❖ Your Exit Strategy

2. Identify, research, and understand the party with which you are negotiating.

   - Who are the players?

   - How many others will you negotiate with?

   - Who are the decision makers?

   - What goals and needs do the other party have?

   - Why are they negotiating?

   - What is their style?

   - What are their personalities?

   - What are their stress points?

   - What negotiation goals do they have?.

   - Are they the only party with whom you could negotiate?

     o Why them?

     o What do they bring to the table?

   - What is the other party's negotiation style?

   - What are their negotiation tactics?

➢ What are your reactions to the tactics?

➢ Has this party negotiated with you before?

    o If so, review the notes from those negotiations.

    o If not, brainstorm with your team and review other negotiations you led.

—

Note: You must know all these items for yourself and your team.

CHAPTER VIII:

THE IMPORTANCE OF QUESTIONS

25+ Power Questions

1. What are the bargaining points in this negotiation?

2. What does the other party value in this negotiation?

3. What is their (or your) preferred outcome?

4. Which bargaining points are more important?

5. Why?

    a. Please explain your position.

    b. Please explain its importance to you.

    c. What facts and figures support your position?

6. How can we validate your position?

7. What are the alternatives to the desired outcome?

8. How do you view our relationship?

   a. Is it transactional?

   b. Is it long term?

9. Who is part of your team?

10. Who is the decision maker?

    a. You?

    b. Your team?

    c. Someone else?

11. How do you arrive at decisions?

12. What resources do you use or need?

13. What steppingstones define the negotiation for you?

14. How will you know that a steppingstone is complete?

15. What alternatives do you see to each steppingstone?

16. Is there one specific way to achieve the steppingstone?

17. Do alternate ways to reach the steppingstone exist?

18. What are the upsides of the steppingstone?

19. What are the downsides of the steppingstone?

20. What do you view as the biggest challenge?

21. What is the worst that can happen in this negotiation?

22. What is the best outcome for this negotiation?

23. What is the best and/or fastest way to arrive at an agreement?

24. Are there any possibilities for delays?

    a. If so, what are they?

    b. Do you have a contingency plan to address them, should they arise?

    c. What would you need to resolve them?

25. How do you measure success?

These power questions address the other party's modus operandi, negotiating position, wherewithal, and motivation. Ask yourself the same questions for at least two reasons: to understand your own position, biases, and negotiation style, and to help answer these questions in case the other party poses them. The questions also facilitate understanding the moving pieces of negotiations and as a starting point for negotiation-appropriate research, plus for preparing for successful negotiations. The better prepared a negotiation party, the more skilled and the more likely positioned for success that party is.

A quick word about skills: they count.

Acquisition of skills is a process that melds knowledge, education, experience, and continuous practice. Often, the more skilled a person is, the easier his or her work and the process appear to others. That is why former FBI hostage negotiator Christopher Voss states that *the most dangerous negotiation is the one you don't know you're in.*

Regarding the power questions listed above, they open the gates to dialogue between the parties, but any skilled negotiator can take them much deeper with additional questions. Deeper questions help in gaining insight into a person's thought process and help in understanding their rationale.

Such questions might include:

- How is that so?

- How did you arrive at your position?

- Why is that important?

- Could you explain this in more detail, please?

- When would you do [fill in the blank]?

- What other parts are important?

- What else do you think I should know?

Skilled negotiators start a conversation that seeks to understand the other party and its position. Such a conversation is about building trust, something that requires active listening, trusting one's gut, and meeting the other party on its level, something that does not mean staying on this level. The dialogue must develop naturally versus firing off question after question from the above list.

Most parties in a negotiation are sensitive to and aware of the other party's approach, authenticity and even its integrity. The party that communicates authenticity will receive the answers it seeks, while one that does not will walk away with little.

It pays to establish trust and to approach negotiations with the other party in mind, instead of declaring war on them. How important that is in real estate negotiations, especially because real estate negotiations traditionally have pitted parties against one another. Anyone negotiating real estate transactions with a more collaborative mindset immediately stands apart. The only word of caution is that the approach must be genuine, lest it backfires.

When determining who is in front of you, these questions also uncover:

- The other party's motivation.

- The other party's legitimate reasons for their position, goals, terms, and conditions.

- Any viable objections they may have.

- Their perception of fairness.

- What they consider reasonable.

- Any items, terms, conditions, etc. that cause concerns for them.

- Anything you may have missed.

As you can tell, questions move negotiations along and the skill level in asking them either makes them effective or not. The questions in this chapter provide ideas about what to ask and how to do it. They are hardly all-inclusive. Besides that, questions should naturally surface in in-depth conversation. Few questions arise in superficial conversations.

The skill of the negotiator often correlates to the questions asked, but skilled negotiators also are cognizant of asking the right questions in the right circumstance of the right party at the right time. This means skilled negotiators ask questions when appropriate versus just asking questions to ask questions. The most valuable tip to remember, then, is to assess the situation and other the parties. You will gain respect and trust when proceeding this way without annoying the other party.

Therefore, consider this section a stimulus. Ask the questions that fit the negotiations in which you find yourself. Many types of questions exist. A quick categorization follows here:

Open-ended questions.

- Questions that require details versus yes or no answers.

- Open-ended questions that encourage respondents to share their views.

- As in "what do you think of this option as a solution?"

Leading Questions

- Leading questions suggest a particular answer.

- As in "Isn't it true that...?" or "You still do [fill in the blank], don't you?"

- Leading questions can carry emotional charge.

- They may be yes or no questions, though not always.

- Discerning a leading question can be difficult. To do so, you must understand the question's intent, frame of reference, and its aim.

Low Key Questions

- Low-key questions are questions that do not trigger emotional responses.

- Example: "If you saw a single-family home and a mansion at the same price, which one would you choose?"

Sequential Questions

- Sequential questions—asking 3 or more questions requiring yes or no answers - are facilitation tools which help uncover potential issues or conflicts.

- Examples: "Do you believe there is sufficient communication in [fill in the blank]?" "Do you think this process is the right one?," ~ "Do you think you are adequately prepared for dealing with [fill in the blank]?"

Questions that Gauge Emotions

- Emotionally gauging questions assess how the other party manages its own emotions and deals with the emotions of others.

- These questions help know the other party much better. They are about emotional intelligence. They also help in diffusing emotional issues that can derail negotiations.

- Examples: "Tell me about how you previously addressed [fill in the blank]?" ~ "Tell me about how you deal with mistakes?" ~ "How do you establish trust?"

Naturally, several other question types can trigger emotional responses. These questions may fall under several of the above categories. Their intent distinguishes them. For example, one might ask questions aggressively. Or one might ask loaded questions, impulsive questions, questions that are tricky and contain innuendo, or questions that trigger emotions.

Unless you aim to put the other party in a defensive spot, want to offend them, or want to obfuscate your meaning, stay away from these questions. They often result in unforeseen actions and reactions, including derailing negotiations, parties walking away, and stalled negotiations. Further, they reveal your personal tendencies, inclinations, and liabilities, and shed a negative light on them.

That said, always think before you speak. It is impossible to take words back. Then, say what you mean, and speak in ways the other party can understand. To do this meticulously prepare, know who you are and what your negotiating style is, and seek to understand rather than being understood. It also bears repeating that active listeners and skilled negotiators possess the ability to adjust their responses, positions, and approaches.

CONCLUSION

A good head and a good heart are always a formidable combination. -- Nelson Mandela.

Real estate negotiating differs from other negotiations. Buying and selling property requires specific details and work. Nevertheless, the actual negotiation process is similar in all negotiations, no matter what the business or the product or service. This book covers the similarities and the differences, but it is tailored to real estate negotiations.

Negotiating is a huge topic which encompasses knowledge, skills, experience from other fields. Those fields include, but are not limited to, psychology, communications, business analysis, law, and the arts. Brilliant negotiators also cultivate wisdom.

As you know, Mother Teresa (1910-1997) was a Catholic nun and missionary, canonized by the Catholic church in 2003. While you likely are aware of her gift of loving the poor, here is what you may not know. She founded and ran a vast enterprise, *The Missionaries of Charity* from 1950 until her death. The organization serves the poor by running and managing orphanages, schools, soup kitchens, clinics, and dispensaries. It is her legacy.

Although *The Missionaries of Charity* generate no profits, the organization always needs to raise funds to continue its work. This work, of course, constituted Mother Teresa's life work and negotiating was an important part of it. Mother Teresa was an excellent negotiator who drove a tough bargain. Her faith, inner attitude, humility, mission, and the work of service resulting from it coalesced. It also inspired her organization.

When she arrived at the negotiating table, often with wealthy, powerful individuals sitting across that table, the first thing she did was smile. She entered the room with a commanding presence, which originated from living what she preached. It was her character that set the tone for the negotiations.

While Mother Teresa had no possessions and no interest in real estate deals, her negotiating style is instructive. She possessed intense focus on accomplishing her mission. Her meticulous preparation, her insight into human nature, and living her life by way of example all distinguish her negotiations. It is hardly a surprise that she achieved what most people consider miracles.

No reader of this book needs to become a Mother Teresa. And yet, readers will do well to study and apply her skills, mindset, and attitude of service in negotiating real estate. That is because all negotiations encompass communications between human beings. Those human beings pursue their own interests and negotiate to arrive at agreements that culminate in contracts. This is as true in real estate negotiations as anywhere else.

All brilliant negotiators understand this. Mary Kay Ash, the founder of the multi-million-dollar *Mary Kay Cosmetics* company, advised: *Never, absolutely never, compromise your principles.*

How important that is!

Yet, the other overarching component to successful negotiations is to put yourself into the other person's shoes. That ensures you understand what that person needs. Although the book details this, it bears repeating that all negotiating parties are human beings.

Of course, you could take pieces and parts of the book and use them in your next negotiation. That is fine, but my advice is to make it your mantra to change yourself, not others. This ensures that the strategies and tactics you may have flipped to before reading anything else have substance when you use them. By doing this one thing, your practice of the principles, fundamentals and applications in this book truly serve you. That is the trajectory that propels you to becoming a skilled negotiator. All else flows from it.

Last, this book aims to equip you with an overview and with tools for negotiating real estate. It is not an end-all and therefore not comprehensive. The book's examples come from my negotiating experience as a long-time real estate professional and from learning from those before me. You will add your own skills, experiences, and wisdom as you travel the path. But now you have a blueprint to negotiate real estate. To your success!

~~~~~~~

Please consider reviewing this book on your favorite platform. I sincerely appreciate it.

GLOSSARY

This glossary refers to common real estate and contract terms. It is not all-inclusive.

Note that many of the terms in this glossary have legal definitions which extend beyond the scope of this book. If you need further clarification and counsel, consult an attorney with expertise in real estate.

Acceptance Expressed written intent of the party receiving an offer to adhere to the terms of the offer. Usually, time limits and specific methods of acceptance apply.

Addendum Document containing additional information, stipulations and terms applicable to the contract. Becomes part of the contract.

Agency Relationship created via a contract or law where one party acts on behalf of another party. The relationship is fiduciary in nature.

Agreement of sale see *Contract*

Apartments see *Multi-Family*

Appraisal A property value estimate or opinion report by a licensed appraiser.

Appreciation Increase of an asset's value.

Arbitration A process involving a neutral third party to resolve disputes between parties. Decisions are final.

Arm's length transaction Refers to the contractual parties' dealing from equal bargaining positions.

As-is condition Contract clause which means the property is sold in its current condition without warranties. The seller will not pay for any repairs.

Asset Piece of property or resource with economic value.

Assignment Transfer of ownership or of rights, liabilities, etc. via a contract.

Back up offer An offer on a property that already has an accepted offer in place – made and accepted in case the accepted offer does not perform or terminates.

Bargaining	Haggling over price and terms to arrive at an agreement.
Breach	Non-performance.
Broker Price Opinion (BPO)	A written value opinion of a property done by a licensed professional (broker).
California Association of Realtors (CAR)	Real estate trade association in California.
Capitalization Rate (CAP Rate)	Equals net operating income divided by sales price. Used to assess potential rate of return of a real estate investment.
Cash flow	Net amount an entity receives and disburses during an accounting period.
CC&Rs	Covenants, Conditions and Restrictions. A legal document controlling the use, restrictions, and requirements of a property.
Closing Costs	Fees that apply to finalizing a loan on a property, e.g. appraisal, title insurance, document, loan origination fees etc.
Competent party	A party that possesses legal capacity to enter a binding contract.

Conditional sales contract	Contract in which the seller retains title to the sold item (security interest) and in which the buyer has equitable interest.
Contingency	Condition that must be met before a contract becomes binding.
Conversions	A process that changes property into a different property class as from single-family homes to multi-family units.
Commercial real estate	offers investors many niche markets, such as large apartment buildings (6+ units), office buildings, industrial condos and buildings, hotels, and retail buildings. Huge variety exists within each category.
Comparables (Comps)	Recently sold or listed properties with similar characteristics and in similar locations to the property you are analyzing.
Condo	Specific unit in a building to which their owner or owners receive title and ownership rights. May have residential, commercial, or industrial zoning.

Consideration   Something of value that establishes a contractual obligation.

Contract   A legally binding agreement between parties.

Cooling off period   see *Recission*

Cooperative   Form of multiple ownership in which a corporation or business trust entity holds title to a property and grants occupancy rights to shareholders.

Counteroffer   Response to an offer received from an offeror.

Damages   An award paid to a party as compensation for loss or injury. Damages can be actual and/or consequential.

Deed   A written instrument by which title to land is transferred.

Development   is the generic term for anything from re-zoning to building new buildings of all types (e.g. condos, apartments, retail, office, mixed-use, and the list goes on).

Disclosures   Statements of fact required by law – see RESPA.

Duress	Unlawful force or action designed to coerce the other party to perform a certain way. Contracts arrived at under duress are not enforceable.
Earnest money	Good-faith deposit (consideration) made by a prospective property buyer. Communicates intent to complete the transaction.
Equitable conversion	Gives the buyer title to a property (for certain purposes) before the closing date.
Equity	The amount of interest or value a property owner holds in a property.
Escalation clause	Contract provision that permits adjustment of certain payments, either up or down.
Escape clause	Contract provision that relieves a party of liability from failure to perform.
Escrow	Procedure in which a third party facilitates buyer's and seller's instructions and handles paperwork and distributes funds.
Eviction	Legal process of removing a tenant because of breaching the lease.
Executed contract	A fully performed contract.

Extension	Agreement to extend a contractual performance period.
Fee Simple	An estate in which the owner has unrestricted power to dispose of property as he wishes. Represents greatest interest a person can have in real estate.
Fiduciary	Persons or entity entrusted with power or property to benefit another party.
Foreclosure	Act of taking possession of a property on which a mortgagee has defaulted.
Forfeiture	Loss of a right or rights as a result of non-performance.
Fraud	Crime using dishonest methods to take items of value from another.
Good faith	An act done Bona Fide, e.g. honestly. Also applies to intent.
Hold harmless clause	Contract provision that indemnifies and protects a party from injuries or lawsuits arising from a particular transaction.
Home Owner's Association (HOA)	Non-profit member association in line with a property's CC&Rs.

Implied contract	An unwritten contract, usually arising from certain conduct of the parties. Note: difficult to prove and enforce.
Land trust	Legal agreement in which a property owner transfers the property to a trustee via a trust agreement.
Lease	Agreement transferring the right of possession of real estate for a specific period of time.
Lease option	Lease clause conveying the right to purchase a property under certain conditions.
Leverage	The ability to generate a larger rate of return with little of one's own money and through borrowed funds instead.
Liquidated Damages	A predetermined amount or percentage an injured party receives if the other party breaches the contract.
Lis Pendens	Recorded legal document that provides notice that a legal action has been filed against a property.
Market Value	Value that represents the most probable price for a property in a competitive and open market.
Mediation	An alternate process to arbitration and often the first step in dispute and conflict resolution. Contrary to arbitration, results are not binding.

Mobile Homes	Prefabricated housing unit attached to land semi permanently.
Modular homes	(tiny homes) Prefabricated housing, often considered personal property.
Multi-Family	are residential rental properties where the actual apartment building size can vary considerably. Location, apartment building size, layouts, amenities, and age break down into further classifications.
Multiple Listing Service (MLS)	Services real estate brokers offer to disseminate property information and establish contractual compensation offers for other brokers.
National Association of Realtors	National real estate trade association in the United States.
Negotiation	Process of reaching an agreement. The act of bargaining.
NNN Lease (triple net lease)	Lease in which the tenant pays rent and all operating expenses.
Non-recourse loan	Loan in which the lender can pursue the property the loan is for only and cannot go after other assets of the borrower.
Note	A debt instrument (promissory note, mortgage note)

Planned Unit Development	refers to a zoning designation for residential, commercial, or industrial property developed at the same or slightly greater overall density than conventional development.
Probate	Process establishing the validity of a will and then administering it.
Reciprocity	Practice or behavior for mutual benefit.
Recission	Cancellation.
Recourse loan	A loan which allows the lender to pursue other borrower assets in addition to the loan collateral.
Release	Relieves a party from any further legal obligation.
Renegotiation	Process that negotiates an agreement anew.
Rent control	Local or state government regulations which stipulate amounts of rent landlords can charge their tenants.
REO	see *foreclosure*
RESPA (Real Estate Settlement Procedures Act)	Federal statute aiming to regulate informing consumers about mortgage settlement costs.

Risk of loss	Contractual terms used to determine which party is responsible for damage after the sale but before delivery.
Seller financing	A loan provided by the seller.
Short sale	Occurs when a property's sale will net less than amounts owed to the lender.
Single-Family Homes	comprise either attached or detached homes, generally built for families and usually one- or two-story homes.
Specific performance	Court-ordered action to compel a party to fulfill the terms of the contract.
Straw man	A dummy purchaser – conceals the identity of the real purchaser.
Subdivision	Tract, lot, or parcel division into more sites for the purpose of development or sale.
'Subject to'	Contract clause which specifies a special condition or contingency that applies to the sale.

Tenancy in Common (TIC)	Joint ownership of property by two or more persons. No right of survivorship.
Time is of the essence	Contractual clause emphasizing the punctual competition of the contractual requirements.
Title	Document that provides evidence of a person's interest or right in a property.
Turnkey	A product or property ready for immediate use.
Underwriting	Lender analysis of the assumed risk in connection to a loan.
Unimproved property	Land without buildings or other improvements
Upgrades	Usually refers to property improvements made after the contract is signed but before the transaction closing date.
Vacancy factor	Estimated vacancy allowance.
Variance	Zoning deviation request to zoning authorities which can grant it.
Void	Null. Not enforceable.

Voidable

May refer to a contract that appears valid and enforceable but that can be voided. For example, due to duress or undue influence.

Waiver

Voluntary surrender of a right.

Zoning

Regulation of structures and uses certain zones or districts.

APPENDIX A

Resources

Mediate   www.mediate.com   everything mediation

Leanin   www.leanin.org   offers negotiation advice for women

Forbes   Business Magazine   www.forbes.com

Harvard Program on Negotiation www.pon.harvard.edu

American Arbitration Association   www.adr.org

National Association of Certified Mediators
https://www.mediatorcertification.org/

National Association of REALTORS® www.nar.realtor

Seek out state and local associations for additional resources.

Do a Google search for "negotiation" and "negotiation training."

A slew of information, consultancies and law firms will appear in the results.

History offers many examples of great negotiators. They include Thucydides, Elizabeth I, Nelson Mandela, Henry Kissinger, Mahatma Gandhi, Nancy Pelosi and many more.

If this short list inspires you, start reading biographies and articles about people who interest you and pay attention to their philosophies, convictions, communication, and personal styles.

Real Estate Contracts

Many types of real estate contracts exist for specific transaction types in residential and commercial real estate transactions. Although this book discusses real estate contracts in some detail, familiarize yourself with the contracts the real estate association in your state uses.

In California, the California Association of Realtors (CAR) contract is in wide use.

However, some cities' and counties' real estate associations, such as San Francisco, offer their member realtors® the use of a San Francisco-specific contract. Most San Francisco realtors® insist on using that contract as it addresses codes, rules, regulations, and issues specific to the city. Other localities may have their own contracts in place, so find out for the place you want to buy, sell, or invest in property. You could start with a call to a local realtor® or the local real estate association.

The internet offers variations on real estate contracts that lack the official vetting and support of real estate associations. Use them at your own risk. Better yet, engage a real estate attorney to assess how solid they are and whether they will serve you well. Naturally, this takes time and money.

Always know and understand the contract and what it contains.

SELECTED BIBLIOGRAPHY

Many books about negotiation exist, fewer about real estate investing.

Not all are listed here.

Altman, Josh. The Altman Close Million-Dollar Negotiation Tactics from America's Top Real Estate Agent. Hoboken, NJ: Wiley, 2019.

Bartsche, Christine. "10 Real Estate Negotiation Tactics to Sell Your House from a Position of Power." Home Light, 2019. https://www.homelight.com/blog/real-estate-negotiation-tactics/.

Berges, S. (2004a). *The Complete Guide to Buying and Selling Apartment Buildings* (2 edition). Hoboken, N.J: Wiley.

Berges, S. (2004b). *The Complete Guide to Real Estate Finance for Investment Properties: How to Analyze Any Single-*

Family, Multifamily, or Commercial Property (1 edition). Hoboken, N.J: Wiley.

Burrell, Tim. Create a Great Deal the Art Real Estate Negotiating; Don't Go to Battle! Learn to Negotiate Gracefully and Make More Money. Columbia, MD: Silloway Pr., 2009.

Carnegie, Dale. *How to Win Friends & Influence People.* New York: Pocket Books, 1998.

Cialdini, Robert. *Influence: The Art and Science of Persuasion.* New York: William Morrow and Company, 1984.

Collins, N., & Collins, A. (2018). *The Savvy Seller: Use Seller Financing to Sell Your Property for Top Dollar and Receive Income for Life* (1 edition). CreateSpace Independent Publishing Platform.

Contributing Editor John W. Reilly with Marie S. Spodek, G. R. I. *Language of Real Estate.* 7th edition. La Crosse, WI: DF Institute, Inc. d/b/a Dearborn Real Estate Educ, 2013.

Cordell, Andrea. *The Negotiation Handbook.* 2nd edition. London ; New York: Routledge, 2018.

Crook, D. (2006). *The Wall Street Journal. Complete Real-Estate Investing Guidebook.* New York: Crown Business.

Davidds, Yasmin, and Ann Bidou. *Your Own Terms: A Woman's Guide to Taking Charge of Any Negotiation.* First edition. New York: AMACOM, 2015.

Dellitt, Julia. "5 Things to Negotiate When You Buy Your First House." Forbes, 2018. https://www.forbes.com/sites/juliadellitt/2018/06/20/5-things-to-negotiate-when-you-buy-your-first-house/#189e53d32d0e.

Fernandez, E. (2016). *1031 Exchanges Made Easy.* CreateSpace Independent Publishing Platform.

Fisher, Roger, and Daniel Shapiro. Beyond Reason: Using Emotions as You Negotiate. New York, NY: Penguin Books, 2006.

Fisher, Roger, Bruce Patton, and William Ury. Getting to Yes: Negotiating Agreement without Giving In. Winnipeg, Canada: Media Production Services Unit, Manitoba Education, 2013.

Fitzgerald, Will. "9 Surprising Tips to Use When Negotiating Real Estate." Raleigh Realty Homes, 2020.

https://www.raleighrealtyhomes.com/blog/negotiate-on-home.html.

Gates, Steve. *The Negotiation Book: Your Definitive Guide To Successful Negotiating*. 1st edition. Chichester: Wiley, 2011.

Graham J.L., Lawrence L., Requejo W.H. (2014) Going Forward to the Past: A Brief History of Negotiation. In: Inventive Negotiation. Palgrave Macmillan, New York.

Greene, Robert, and Joost Elffers. The 48 Laws of Power. London, UK: Profile Books, 2015.

Hennessey, B. (2015b). *The Due Diligence Handbook for Commercial Real Estate: A Proven System To Save Time, Money, Headaches And Create Value When Buying Commercial Real Estate* (Second edition). United States: CreateSpace Independent Publishing Platform.

Horn, J. S. (n.d.). *The ABC's of 1031 Exchanges and Triple Net Lease Properties*.

Heus, Geurt Jan de. *Mastering the Art of Negotiation: Seven Guides for Creating Your Journey*. Laurence King Publishing, 2017.

Horton, Simon. *The Leader's Guide to Negotiation: How to Use Soft Skills to Get Hard Results.* Pearson Education, 2016.

Jones, Phil M., Chris Smith, and Jimmy Mackin. Exactly What to Say for Real Estate Agents: The Magic Words for Influence and Impact. Hoboken, NJ: Box of Tricks/Page Two Books, 2019.

Keller, G., Jenks, D., & Papasan, J. (2005). *The Millionaire Real Estate Investor* (1 edition). New York: McGraw-Hill Education.

Lake, L. J. (2015). *Seller Financing: Real Estate Investing for Anyone.* Vassar International Publishing.

Lantrip, M. (2017). *How to Do A Section 1031 Like Kind Exchange: Simultaneous, Delayed, Reverse, Construction* (1.0 edition). Anderson Logan, LLC.

Lindahl, D. (2008). *Multi-Family Millions: How Anyone Can Reposition Apartments for Big Profits* (1 edition). Hoboken, N.J: Wiley.

Malhotra, Deepak, and Max H. Bazerman. Negotiation Genius: How to Overcome Obstacles and

Achieve Brilliant Results at the Bargaining Table and Beyond. New York, NY: Batam Books, 2008.

Manganelli, B. (2014). *Real Estate Investing: Market Analysis, Valuation Techniques, and Risk Management* (2015 edition). New York: Springer.

McElroy, K. (2012b). *The ABCs of Real Estate Investing: The Secrets of Finding Hidden Profits Most Investors Miss* (Reprint edition). Minden, NV: RDA Press, LLC.

Murad, Andrea. "11 Things You Need to Know About Real Estates Negotiations." Entrepreneur, 2016. https://www.entrepreneur.com/article/253732.

Owusu-Ansah, A. (2018). *Construction and Application of Property Price Indices* (1 edition). Abingdon, Oxon ; New York, NY: Routledge.

Patterson, Kerry, Joseph Grenny, Ron McMillan, and Al Switzler. Crucial Conversations Tools for Talking When Stakes Are High. New York, NY: McGraw-Hill, 2012.

Pivar, William H., and Richard W. Post. *Power Real Estate Negotiation*. Real Estate Education Company, 1990.

Poorvu, W. J., & Cruikshank, J. L. (1999a). *The Real Estate Game: The Intelligent Guide To Decisionmaking And Investment*. New York, NY: Free Press.

Requejo, William Hernández, and John L. Graham. *Global Negotiation: The New Rules*. Illustrated edition. New York: St. Martin's Press, 2008.

Rosen, K. D. (2017). *Investing in Income Properties: The Big Six Formula for Achieving Wealth in Real Estate* (2 edition). Hoboken: Wiley.

Schaub, J. (2016). *Building Wealth One House at a Time, Updated and Expanded, Second Edition* (2 edition). New York: McGraw-Hill Education.

Scott, J. "How to Negotiate: 7 Real Estate Negotiation Tips." BiggerPockets, 2016. · https://www.biggerpockets.com/blog/2010-03-24-7-tips-for-better-real-estate-negotiation.

Scott, J., Mark Ferguson, and Carol Scott. *The Book on Negotiating Real Estate: Expert Strategies for Getting the Best Deals When Buying & Selling Investment Property*. Denver, CO: BiggerPockets Publishing, 2019.

Sivori, R. J., & P, F. (2017). *Creative Real Estate Financing: Seller / Buyer Win! Win!* (1 edition). CreateSpace Independent Publishing Platform.

Smith, Arthur D. Howden. John Jacob Astor: Landlord of New York. New York, NY: Cosimo Classics, 2005.

Subramanian, Guhan. *Dealmaking: The New Strategy of Negotiauctions (First Edition): New Dealmaking Strategies for a Competitive Marketplace.* 01 edition. W. W. Norton & Company, 2010.

Sutherland, C. (2015). *Creative Real Estate Seller Financing: How to Use Seller Financing to Buy or Sell Any Real Estate.* CES Sutherland Management LLC.

Sutton, G. (2013). *Loopholes of Real Estate.* Scottsdale, AZ: RDA Press, LLC.

Trump, Donald, and Tony Schwartz. Trump: The Art of the Deal. New York, NY: Ballantine Books, 2015.

Ury, William. Getting Past No: Negotiating in Difficult Situations. New York, NY: Bantam Books, 2007.

Voss, Chris Never Split the Difference: Negotiating as If Your Life Depended on It. London: Random House Business Books, 2016.

Walch, Karen S., Stephan M. Mardyks, Joerg Schmitz, and Michael Wheeler. *Quantum Negotiation: The Art of Getting What You Need*. 1st edition. Hoboken, New Jersey: Wiley, 2017.

Willerton, Dale, and Jeff Grandfield. *Negotiating Commercial Leases & Renewals For Dummies*. John Wiley & Sons, 2013.

Woolley, T., & Porritt, J. (2006). *Natural Building: A Guide to Materials and Techniques*. Ramsbury: Crowood Press.

"The Natural History of Negotiation and Mediation: The Evolution of Negotiative Behaviors, Rituals, and Approaches," October 31, 2020. https://www.mediate.com/articles/NaturalHistory.cfm.

INDEX

ACKNOWLEDGEMENTS

Any book, including this one, comprises many facets and requires a great team. I am indebted to colleagues, whether real estate professionals, attorneys, or other professionals. I am grateful to my clients for teaching me (almost) everything I know.

My research assistant Emma Graham did a stellar job before she departed for her dream career in New York City. Beyond that, life is an outstanding teacher, as are other people. I am grateful to all.

ABOUT THE AUTHOR

Gabrielle Dahms is a real estate investor, broker, and writer who also holds a master's in history. She has published hundreds of articles and blog posts about real estate and how to invest in real estate for over 17 years. She is an avid traveler, speaks three languages, loves yoga, and lives in San Francisco.

Gabrielle Dahms es inversora inmobiliaria, agente inmobiliaria y escritora que también tiene una maestría en historia. Ha publicado cientos de artículos y entradas en blogs sobre bienes raíces y cómo invertir en bienes raíces por más de 17 años. Es una viajera ávida, habla tres idiomas, le encanta el yoga y vive en San Francisco.

Gabrielle Dahms ist Immobilieninvestorin, Immobilienmaklerin und Schriftstellerin, die außerdem einen Magister Abschluss in Geschichte besitzt. Sie hat seit über 17 Jahren Hunderte von Artikeln und Blogbeiträgen über Immobilien und wie man in Immobilieninvestiert, veröffentlicht. Sie ist eine begeisterte Reisende, spricht drei Sprachen, liebt Yoga und lebt in San Francisco.

Book a Consultation with Gabrielle Dahms

Or

Order a Personalized Masterplan for your real estate investing needs.

Or

Book Gabrielle as a speaker for your next webinar, conference, or event.

Send an email with your request to realestatemanuals@gmail.com.

Briefly state your contact details (name, address, phone number, email), what you need and indicate your budget.

Thank you!

Made in the USA
Columbia, SC
05 April 2021

35666166R00129